THE UNVEILING
OF YOUR SOUL PATH

Earlier publications by the authors:

Spirituele Relaties (Spiritual Relationships)
De Hemel binnen Handbereik (Heaven within Reach)
De Ontsluiering van je Zielenpad (The Unveiling of Your Soul Path)
Gevoelens verwoorden maakt je vrij (Expressing Your Feelings Sets You Free)
Maak je Hemel op Aarde (Create Your Own Heaven on Earth)
De DNA Code van de Ziel (The DNA Code of Your Soul)
Het Kosmische plan van de Nieuwe Tijd (The Cosmic Plan of the New Age)
Sleutels tot Geluk (Keys to Happiness)
De dag waarop mijn Ziel in opstand kwam (The Day My Soul Rose Up)
Wat Zoekers neit vinden en Vinders niet zoeken (What Seekers Don't Find and Finders Don't Seek)

The Anthony Symbol is the symbol for the Centre for Spiritual Insight. It has a very specific meaning. The cross stands for the material – you live on earth and there is a reason for this. The outer circle stands for the Greater Oneness and makes you aware that you are part of this. In the centre of all of this, the little globe, that's where you are.

Much love, strength and wisdom.

www.thesiranthonyfoundation.org
www.centrumvoorspiritueelinzicht.org

THE UNVEILING OF YOUR SOUL PATH

Progressive Insights
Into The DNA Code Of Your Soul

Boudewijn Donceel - William Gijsen

Published by Uitgeverij The Sir Anthony Foundation -
Private Stichting

Publisher: The Sir Anthony Foundation - Private Stichting

Hamonterweg 133, 3950 Bocholt, Belgium

Telephone: +32 11 44 81 19

Mail: william@williamgijsen.org
boudewijn@boudewijndonceel.org

Website: www.thesiranthonyfoundation.org
www.centrumvoorspiriuteelinzicht.org

Printing and binding: Print On Demand
Original title: De Ontsluiering van je Zielenpad
Translation: Lynn Coleman
Background for cover: Elly Munten
Cover design, editing, layout and graphical design:
The Sir Anthony Foundation - Private Stichting
Authors: Boudewijn Donceel, William Gijsen

Copyright (c) 2017 Uitgeverij The Sir Anthony Foundation - Private Stichting, Bocholt, Belgium, William Gijsen, Bocholt, Belgium, Boudewijn Donceel, Bocholt, Belgium.

All rights reserved. No part of this publication may be reproduced, stored or made public in any form or by any means, printing, photocopying, digital systems, or otherwise, without the prior written permission of the publisher.

ISBN 9789492340047

NUR 720, NUR2 728

TABLE OF CONTENTS

FOREWORD	7
THE MEANING OF YOUR EXISTENCE	9
BIRTH MISSION	20
Sphere Behaviour	24
Basic Profile: Finders and Seekers	30
Types: Thinker, Doer, Feeler	33
Meditation	37
Birth Code	41
Age Code	55
RELATIONSHIP MISSION	60
Mars & Venus Code	62
Q-Code	78
Z-Code	84
C-Code & Sphere Fear	90
EVOLUTION MISSION	94
PERSONAL SOUL MISSION	104
CLEANSING BALLAST	109
Cleansing Karma	111
Cleansing fears	124
Cleansing Rational Fallacies	127
Cleansing your Ego	132
Intentions	136
Body and Soul	145
Refusal	148
DEGREES OF TRANSFORMATION	153
1st Degree of Transformation: BEING Aware	156

2nd Degree of Transformation: Consulting Your Conscience	158
3rd Degree of Transformation: Acceptance Degree	159
4th Degree of Transformation: Freedom Degree	161
5th Degree of Transformation: Creation Degree	163
6th Degree of Transformation: Meditation Degree	167
7th Degree of Transformation: Surrender Degree	168
Example	169
What Do I Want?	177
RECOGNISING YOUR SOUL FEELING	182
9 MILESTONES	187
Children, 0 to 12	188
Adolescence, 12 to 18	190
Adult, 18 to 50	192
Work	197
Relationship	199
Divorcing or Releasing	201
Fifty +	203
Seventy +	204
Life's End	205
EPILOGUE	208
OVERVIEW OF CHARACTERISTICS	209
THE CENTRE FOR SPIRITUAL INSIGHT	234

FOREWORD

Greetings Dear Reader,

My name is Anthony van Dijck. At least, that's the name that I'm using here, because I've had several names over several lifetimes. Does that surprise you? I'll give you more explanation about this later in the book.

The same is true for you as well. You too have had several lives before now. Exciting, isn't it? Are you prepared to accept this premise? Then you're now at the start of an inspiring story, which will teach you more about yourself.

I am a higher Soul. My mission is to explain the workings of the Greater Oneness and your place in this whole as well. The Soul is the foundation for this; it gives you a totally new look at life.

Over the last 15 years I've transferred a lot of information about the Soul Path, step by step. I wish to bundle all this knowledge into one book. It's very important to me that it will be made available for whoever is open to it.

Why? Because the time is ripe. People are looking for their Soul Path more than ever now. That fits the current Zeitgeist. We've arrived in an era of raised consciousness, many are awakening and asking questions about themselves.

Call it the awakening of the Soul. However, finding your own life path is a difficult task. There's a personal map to do this, but it's difficult to read without guidance. That's why it's good to have complete instructions about how to read the map.

The DNA Code of Your Soul is the legend belonging to your map. It clarifies where you currently are and the circumstances with which you are confronted. Your DNA Code is a complete set of personal characteristics, your Soul Characteristics.

Searching for your path on the map is a matter of trial and error, you learn from experience, from being aware of yourself and from enquiring into yourself.

You find your path by first experiencing life lessons and then applying these in practise. That's real spirituality.

There are, of course, obstacles on the way, hurdles which keep you away from your own true self. You learn to go through these by trial and error too. It's also necessary to know your map here, so that you can learn to deal with them and to clear away ballast.

Your path can become a lot easier and more comprehensible and recognizable in this way. The central key is developing your consciousness. You can only change something which you are aware of. Take it from me, you are acting more unconsciously than consciously.

You also need to answer the most important life question of all: where does my path lead to? If you don't know where you are going, then you can never find the right way. What's the meaning of life, the point of your existence?

Unveiling your Soul Path is a breath-taking and dizzying journey. In this book, I'll tell you how you can find and follow your path. It's a tough nut to crack and it might be difficult to digest in one go. It might even make your head spin. That will be a good moment to let what you have just been reading sink in.

Unveiling your Soul Path requires a step by step approach. Even so, I want to tell this story as a whole. It's necessary and important to make it available in its entirety. See it as the Bible of the New Age, the instructions to unveil your Soul Path.

Anthony Van Dijck

THE MEANING OF YOUR EXISTENCE

Unveiling your Soul Path gives you the meaning for your existence. You start looking for your path in each and every life. That's because you are here with a specific mission. Deep inside you can feel it, at least if you are open to the idea.

The key lies with becoming and being conscious. You have a free choice in this. The masses choose aimlessness, but the group that is looking for the meaning of their existence and which experiences that there is more between Heaven and Earth than just the material, is visibly growing.

Step by step I'll unveil your Soul Path and make it comprehensible, so that you can learn to find your own path.

So, what is your Soul? Does it really exist? What is there apart from the material? Is there more than we can perceive through our own senses? How can I know that for sure?

These are some of the questions that many people ask. I can summarise the answers as follows, as being in essence:

Your Soul is immortal, immaterial, invisible, but can be felt in all of us. Why should you believe that? Well, your believing can become knowing if you are open to it.

A first approach is a proof from absurdity. Without your Soul's existence, life would be pointless. You may experience a voice deep inside you which says that this pointlessness isn't right. You experience an inner prompting through which you have no choice but to develop your conscience. Throughout your life you grow in wisdom. This is called maturity.

This doesn't, of course, provide any scientific proof for the existence of the Soul, but it is a plausible explanation for now. Know that by pausing to contemplate your own experiences, that your own 'science of self' develops. This means that you don't have to take on anything without questioning; it is a conscious choice to develop your consciousness.

Without allowing for the existence of your Soul, many

questions remain unanswered. If you dare to assume its existence as a starting point, a stunning picture emerges which explains everything.

Why shouldn't this be true? Maybe until the opposite has been proved. Admittedly, it's human to have doubts, it's even part of your path. So, feel what you feel inside at every experience, deal with your doubts and learn from experience. In this way, you develop your own wisdom.

Feelings are the language of your Soul. This is the complete opposite of what you have learned during your upbringing and at school. There it was all about rational and analytical approaches, learning to behave according to the norm. Intuition and spontaneity don't really fit into that picture. Over the years we have unlearned how to feel.

You will certainly have experienced a practical example of how your Soul works. If you meet someone for the first time and shake their hand, you'll immediately get a feeling about them, they're ok or they're not ok. That is your intuition giving you reliable information.

Your intuition is the Soul's sense, so it's important to learn how to use this sense and to develop it. Straightaway, this is an important part of finding your life path.

That's because your gut feelings are a kind of compass which tell you if you want something or not. They differentiate between what suits you and what doesn't. If you know how to use this compass, then you'll automatically find the right path.

A second way to experience the existence of your Soul is via your own DNA Code of the Soul. Your DNA Code shows you your Soul Characteristics. If you request your DNA Code, you will discover that these characteristics fit you.

Maybe you won't comprehend all the aspects straightaway, but you will recognise the main theme. As you become more and more familiar with it, you won't have any doubts any more. This is the most important proof. Your own experience turns believing into knowing.

This also requires you to accept that the Spirit World exists. For we are passing on the Code. This may be the second concept which is difficult to accept. But if you accept that the Soul exists, then it is logical that there's a Spirit World where Souls exist when they are not in the material world. It explains death, birth and incarnations. Deep inside you'll find confirmation that this is the case.

Anyone can make contact with the Spirit World. Know that everyone has a Guide supporting them from the Spirit World. See them as guardian angels. They guide you through the unveiling of your Soul Path, but only if you want them to. There is no force involved, it's always your own free choice.

Can I find out my Soul Characteristics myself from my guardian angel? Sorry, that's not possible. You can feel some things intuitively, but passing on Soul Characteristics is a delicate matter. Those of us here in the Spirit World have chosen one channel and not the other way around. That might seem a little dishonest, but dealing with the information which is passed on is a very responsible task and there are not many who are able to do so.

This is a lesson from the past when Jesus tried to unveil the Soul Path. A good deal of misuse was made of that and that resulted in the current church, which is mainly based on power structures. Here in the Spirit World, exercising power is not done. That's why we're very careful about passing on information. We don't want to make the same mistake again.

But now back to the Soul. Where does it come from and where does it want to go? Why does something like a Soul exist? The explanation is simple. The sum of all Souls forms the Greater Oneness. Souls are present in the material world, but a great proportion remain in the Spirit World. Souls incarnate on Earth, to grow in wisdom.

The material world is an ideal environment for the Soul to go through experiences, to learn and to pick up life lessons. Each life makes you a little wiser and that wisdom remains. You take this with you to your next life.

It is a strange fact. On the one hand, you experience your own true self as a Soul, you are an individual. At the same time, you are part of a Greater Oneness, so you are a part of something. It seems contradictory, but throughout the unveiling of your path, your consciousness grows with it.

Later in this book you will learn how to have contact with the Spirit World and to ask it for advice. If you ask the Greater Oneness for advice, you will only receive advice in line with your Soul. That is because there is no difference between what your Soul wants and what the Greater Oneness wants. That's how you are both yourself as well as part of the whole.

But who am I really? Am I my Soul? Or something else? It seems like an inexplicable tangled mess, that can only serve to confuse you. That's why it's so important to see your SELF as the result of your Soul, your past, your anxieties, your Ego, your desires, ...

So, you are a melting pot of lots of things and inside, your Soul strives to find your authentic self, clearing away ballast which stops you being who you really are. Your Soul also wants to grow in wisdom and prevent ballast from increasing. Gaining and applying wisdom is the only real definition of spirituality.

What's the point of that? The explanation can be found in the Aim of the Greater Oneness. This has the primal desire to want to grow in wisdom. We sometimes refer to the Greater Oneness as God. There have been many books written on the subject. Let's provide a simple definition here of God:

> God is the creative force searching for insights.

Do you get this sentence? Take your time to realise what this statement means.

You may recognize this characteristic in yourself. I have already told you that an inner prompting is needed to develop your conscience. So, feel like a speck of God! The primal desire of the Greater Oneness explains your own Soul Wish to want to grow in wisdom. That's because you are part of that whole. You make your contribution by gaining insights.

Once upon a time the Greater Oneness was One. All the Souls were together in the Oneness, with their primal urge to want to grow in wisdom. Then a pretty drastic decision was taken, namely the Big Bang. See it as a free choice of the Oneness to be able to grow. The Big Bang ensured that the Oneness divided into little pieces, with the aim of giving each little piece the chance to grow.

Each one of these little pieces is a Soul. Each little piece follows its own growth path and comes back together in Oneness. Growing is the result of gaining insights, developing your own wisdom. That's how the Greater Oneness grows, as a universal sum of the growth of every individual.

A critical question at this point is if this is right. It seems to be too good to be true. However, your thinking is too limited to be able to comprehend this. Let your knowledge and conscience chew on it. Maybe your inner voice will say that it might well be true. In the material world, everything can be seen in time and space. Your rational mind is insufficient to be able to grasp all of this, so make use of your feelings, they will give you the answers.

Now back to the essence, let's assume you are part of the Greater Oneness. By growing in wisdom, by going through experiences, you can contribute to the Greater Oneness.

You can only gain correct insights by feeling them. Feelings are, as we have said before, the language of your Soul. Along with an insight you gain a feeling of satisfaction. It is an expression of the love for yourself. We'll go into this deeper later.

I primarily want to explain how to find your Soul Path in the material world. However, as this also brings up some questions about the Spirit World, I'll give you some information about that first.

The Spirit World is the place where your Soul resides between two lives. What does a Soul do in the meantime? Well, that depends. Some are recovering from their previous life and resting, others get to work guiding Souls in the material world.

As previously stated, each of you experiences something like a guardian angel. That's a Soul in the Spirit World who's taken it upon themselves to help you. This is a way for this Soul to gain more experiences and to grow as a result.

You can actively call upon this help line, it's a matter of using it. We call your guiding Soul, your Guiding Spirit, Guide or Master. The name itself isn't very important; the main thing is that you are aware of their existence.

Working with your Guide is a win-win situation. A Guide needs your contact with the material world for him to grow. The better you do, the wiser they become.

Another task of the Spirit World is creating coincidences for you. There's actually no such thing as a coincidence. The Spirit World arranges them for you and then offers you the chance to gain a life experience. You have the free will to choose to learn this lesson. If you choose not to, then they'll organise the next opportunity, until you've understood it.

This explains a thing or two. For example, imagine I'm having problems with my boss at work. Is that a coincidence? No, that is a chance to learn how to deal with it. If I decide to change jobs without having learned my lesson, then I'm guaranteed to go through the same problems again with my new boss.

If I've learned this lesson and have grown in wisdom, then I won't need this experience anymore and I'll be presented with the next subject. Then I might be ready for a new job or I won't encounter as many problems in the contact with my boss any more.

The Spirit World acts as an intermediary, to allow you to have the experiences which you need to discover your Soul Path.

The same is true of relationships. The number of divorces is growing dramatically, the lack of satisfaction in relationships keeps increasing. There is nothing wrong with divorce per se, as long you've learned your lesson and approach things differently the next time. Otherwise you'll get into trouble again.

This is how the Spirit World ensures that you deal with your lessons one by one. You can't get going on lesson 5 if you haven't understood lesson 1 yet. That's why people often stay stuck in one stage, which can only be severed through insight.

Lightning never strikes twice, does it? Well, unfortunately that's not true for people making mistakes, they are often busy repeating them.

That doesn't make for good reading, is it? But you know it's true. That's why I'm repeating my plea for being conscious. This prevents repeated mistakes. Deep inside that's what you'd really like, but sometimes you're a little hard of hearing and you don't even listen to yourselves.

Ultimately, you decide yourself if you'd like to learn your lesson or follow the coincidences. That happens if you're ready and it requires an act of will. Living life consciously, following your Soul, is not always easy. But one day you'll take the steps on your path. It's the only way to go and you decide when you are ready to start and how far you want to go.

Doesn't the Spirit World exert any force by creating these coincidences? The answer is no, it offers opportunities to gain insights. This step is a matter of free will. Actually, offering insights is pure love, precisely because there's no compulsion attached. The wish to take it up is an inner choice, a conscious personal step.

So, how do incarnations work? Do they keep going endlessly? Do they ever stop? Well, a Soul can reincarnate more than a thousand times, but at some point, it stops. If you've learned all the lessons in the material world, you won't return. Then you'll stay in the Spirit World to work on your further growth.

What if the growth is finished? Well, gaining wisdom never

actually stops. The growth is endless. It keeps getting more refined and better. You can also guide other Souls with the wisdom you have gained. In this way, the Oneness keeps on growing.

What if the Oneness has completed its growth, will there be the next Big Bang? Well, know that the end of the world is a long way away, we still have millions of years to go. When the earthly project has finished, there may be other ways for the Greater Oneness to grow. You might find that fascinating. But I'll have to disappoint you, for now it is better for you to concentrate on your own Soul instead of worrying about the future of the Greater Oneness.

Let's return to the core of the matter, your own Soul. Your Soul Evolution is a contribution to the Greater Oneness and to what your inner self wishes to achieve. This reflects the meaning of your existence. Through this your life has an aim. You aren't here for nothing. You have the choice to approach your life in a conscious way and so be able to fulfil your deepest inner wishes. The other alternative is to live passively and unconsciously.

Whatever you choose, it doesn't matter, but choosing lack of consciousness is putting off the inevitable path to be followed.

This brings me to your Soul Mission, because this is your instruction for this life. Your previous lives have had a forming influence on it. However, you can't change that. Only this life counts. So, living in the here and now is the only correct motto.

Your Soul Mission is made up of different parts. It's actually quite an extensive story, that you'll only be able to digest if it's broken down into pieces. That's why I'm giving you the following subdivisions for your Soul Mission:

- Birth Mission
- Relationship Mission
- Evolution Mission

- Personal Soul Mission
- Cleansing Karma, dealing with fears, restrictive rationality, Ego
- Achieving milestones

I'll explain all these subjects in more detail in different chapters. To give you an initial insight, I'll summarize them here:

- Your Birth Mission is the sum of characteristics which reflect your true self. Your Soul strives to make this its own and to become wiser step by step. It's specifically to do with the development of yourself, towards yourself.

- Your Relationship Mission shows you characteristics to do with your relationship with others. You can gather a lot of wisdom from this as well. Think about how you are influenced by your environment and how you influence others. The closer people are to you, the greater the impact.

- Your Evolution Mission gives you a third way of growing in wisdom. Here you learn to deal with the various circumstances in which you are carrying out your Birth Mission.

- Your personal Soul Mission is very specific and can consist of many parts. For example, simply learning to stick up for yourself or possibly a higher mission, such as conveying the Message. This mission is partly determined by what you have achieved in previous lives.

- Cleansing Karma is a way of learning lessons and casting off ballast, which makes your life work a lot more easily. Other obstacles from which you can learn lessons are your fears, your rational mind and your Ego. These are unconscious patterns of behaviour. They keep you away from your authentic self, your Soul Path. Learning to deal with them teaches you how to better know your path.

- You do all of this from childhood until your death, through

9 Milestones. They are all part of your Soul Path and consist of specific experiences.

As I already said, this is a lot to digest in one go and you may now not be able to see the wood for the trees. Don't worry about that right now, I'll explain each part as we go, chapter by chapter, bit by bit.

If you start getting confused, take some time to digest what you have read. You can't do everything in one go.

If you really want to work on unveiling your Soul Path, then I would advise you to read the book all the way through, and then to zone in deeper on specific sections.

I can only repeat that it's my deepest wish to bring the overall information together as a whole. See it as a reference book, in which you can consult that part which is important to you at that moment.

Before we go deeper into each section, I'd like to introduce the following subjects:

What is Karma? You may not know the correct meaning. By that I mean, not fate, as in Eastern spirituality, but the ballast which you have accumulated and which is causing havoc for your Soul. This consists of predominantly unspoken and unfelt feelings. That's why you are confronted with coincidences in the here and now, so that you can re-experience these feelings and put them to rest. I'll explain ballast cleansing further in a later chapter.

The DNA Code of your Soul is a manual for becoming yourself in the material world, let's say the search for "external balance". It portrays a series of personal characteristics which you learn to act in accordance with.

The Degrees of Transformation are the way to find your "inner balance". They're the instructions for tackling your problems in seven steps. They help you take hold of your own destiny and to create it, instead of undergoing it.

Finding your inner and external balance, balance between

your male and female sides, between your thinking and feeling, between the material and the spiritual, between power and love are important parts of your Soul Path.

How do you find your balance? There's only one way to do so, namely by a process of trial and error. But with this manual you'll be able to find your feet again more quickly and the errors won't hurt so much!

Recognising your Soul Feeling is crucial in this. How do you know what you really want? Can I feel my Soul? What should I do with all these unpleasant feelings? Why do I have them?

Sensing your compass, intuitive knowing, unveils your path and dissolves the mist surrounding it. It provides clarity about where the path is leading and how to traverse it.

You'll undoubtedly be confronted by your own existential question, who am I? It's a very confusing question. What's leading in who I am? Am I acting according to my Soul, my Ego, my fears, my Karma? You are who you are: the result of all of this.

It's good to understand yourself, however, and to realise which part has the upper hand at which moment. You develop your wisdom throughout your life. You can learn to know yourself better, make a difference and choose what suits you best by the actions you take. This will help you discover the inner strength to want to live in alignment with your Soul. Anything which distracts you from this, you'll find superfluous.

It's important to accept who you are, that's where your path starts. Nobody is perfect, that's not possible. I can only warn you: don't try to be. You'd only be deluding yourself. The only right way to proceed is by being realistic and keeping your feet on the ground. That's the only way that you'll discover who you really are and find your own path.

So, these are the contents of this book. I'll explain each part step by step. It's going to be a long journey, so make sure you take your time. Then it's up to you. Which path will you take?

BIRTH MISSION

You need to be aware that this chapter contains a lot of theory. Manuals have basic information that you need to learn to work with. If you want to learn how to read maps, you need to have some knowledge of the meaning of the legend. Otherwise you'll only be scratching the surface of your path, unconsciously as it were. So, keep your nose to the grindstone for a while, the theory you read here will be very useful to you later.

Before going into your Birth Mission, you need to know the main points of the Soul Evolution on earth throughout your incarnations.

Your growth in the material world consists of 3 x 7 steps, so 21 learning steps in all. Further on, you'll find an overview.

When you've learned all the lessons in a specific part and have learned to apply them, then you go onto the next level.

The first 7 steps are aimed at going through experiences, gathering them. Doing that teaches you to tackle life, to stick up for yourself, to keep going, to confront your environment, to sow and to grow, to learn from your mistakes, to experience emotions and to reject what can't be trusted. We call this the First Sphere.

If you were born as a First Sphere, then that largely determines who you are. Because of your limited life experience, you are focused on others, compliant and dependent.

That changes in the Second Sphere, which also consists of 7 steps. Here, you start looking for your self-reliance, own choices, for what is valuable and you learn to feel. That's how you learn to set your boundaries, to determine what's really important to you, to investigate and to give up your urge to impose.

A Second Sphere is typically strongly individualistic and differentiates what is good for them. Others are secondary.

There's nothing wrong with that as such, but it can go wrong.

Doing this in the wrong way leads to egotism and even fat cat culture. This is something that we have increasingly been having to deal with over the last few decades. That's because the percentage of Second Spheres is increasing. That's why we are noticing it more, but the characteristic has always existed.

The Third Sphere, the last 7 steps, are aimed at elevating yourself and others. After you've learned to distinguish, you want to help yourself and others to develop.

It's important that your offer to help others to develop has no strings attached. You offer your own experience and insights, but with no pressure, because that would go against your Soul.

The Third Sphere teaches you to work together, to share your wisdom, to strive for inner and external balance, to show comprehension in the right way, to passionately follow your Soul, to act in wisdom and knowledge and to surrender unconditionally by accepting what is. Because what is, is good, otherwise it's different!

So, now you have an initial picture of the 21 steps in wisdom, divided up into the 3 related Spheres. These play an important role in unveiling your Soul Path. You'll find out more about this in the chapters to come.

I'll list all these characteristics again on the following page:

THE 21 LEVELS OF WISDOM

<u>1st Sphere – Gathering:</u>

Tackling

Persevering

Confronting

Sowing and growing

Daring to make mistakes

Learning to experience emotions

Giving up what doesn't fit

<u>2nd Sphere – Differentiating:</u>

Making choices

Valuing your possessions and self-worth

Differentiating through feelings

Setting boundaries

Differentiating major and minor issues

Investigating

Letting go the urge to impose

<u>3rd Sphere – Elevating:</u>

Working together

Sharing

Developing your inner balance

Showing comprehension

Passionately elevating

Inner knowing

Unconditional surrender

So, now you have a first general picture of the Soul Evolution, divided up into learning levels. We'll keep coming back to the 21 steps. That's because each of the steps has its own characteristics. These help to form your Birth Mission.

What do we mean with "Birth Mission"? It's the description of your Soul Mission for this life, which refers to yourself.

It tells you which characteristics your Soul is working on in this life. It determines what you are like, but it also includes what you need to learn.

Your Birth Mission consists of the following characteristics:
- Sphere behaviour
- Basic Profile
- Type
- Birth Code
- Age Code

This is the start Code for self-development, see it as the basic characteristics of your Soul. If you want to start unveiling your Soul Path, start by learning about these characteristics and really understanding them.

I can only repeat, it's a lot to digest and you won't be able to force it down in one go. So, start with a small taster. I'll go into each characteristic, step by step, in more depth, take your time for this.

Sphere Behaviour

In the introduction, I've already given you a brief explanation about the Sphere of your birth; this determines your being to an important extent. This translates into a characteristic, namely your Sphere Behaviour.

It's interesting to know that you can implement this characteristic in a positive or negative way. Know that everyone makes mistakes. Incorrectly applying your Sphere Behaviour teaches you how you can do things differently and in a better way. To do that you need to take a look in the mirror, evaluate yourself and to draw lessons from it.

Your Sphere Behaviour tells you in which Sphere you were born, First, Second or Third. In addition, it also tells you how you should apply the numbers in your DNA Code. Your Number Code will be explained later. Your Birth Sphere is indicated by the first figure in your Sphere Step. More explanation about this will follow later.

The Sphere Behaviour is possibly the most underestimated experience you go through on earth in your DNA Code. I often see people focussing on their Number Codes and forgetting to apply their Sphere Behaviour to them.

Applying your Sphere Behaviour is the way you can reach conclusions about how best to implement your DNA Code. See it as the "action part". It's the way in which you apply the Codes to draw lessons from them.

Growing in wisdom is gaining insights from your experiences and from there, applying these conclusions as a guiding theme in your life.

What's typical for a First Sphere? A First Sphere builds their experiences by gathering them. Often, they feel like a victim and they lay the blame for what they experience at someone else's door.

They hesitate to take responsibility for themselves. This is what going through the First Sphere teaches them.

> **1st Sphere:** Gather as many experiences as you can in which you can implement your DNA Code and find insights into these. Your mission is to gather. Be careful, you have the tendency to take on a destructive attitude.

A Second Sphere learns to differentiate between what they want based on feelings, sifting as it were. This doesn't always work out the first time. They learn from a process of trial and error, by absorbing lessons from the mistakes they make.

The ultimate aim of the Second Sphere is to determine through their feelings what really suits them and what doesn't. They are focussed mainly on themselves and, in the first instance, only see one side of the coin.

Previously, I showed you the link to society's growing egotism. You'll be able to see this around you. Many don't know how to deal with this and view it as the loss of traditional values. These traditional values are First Sphere Behaviour: compliance, orderliness and, in particular, not asking any difficult questions.

A Second Sphere wants to construct their own opinions and not just unquestioningly accept what they are being told about themselves. A lot is changing in society because of the increasing number of Second Spheres.

The youth states their opinion more strongly and they have become more assertive. More relationships burst apart, because of prioritising one's own opinion. Motivation also lessens at work, because a Second Sphere acts, in the first instance, for themselves and not for their employer. Second Sphere behaviour spreads into all areas of life.

> **2nd Sphere:** When gathering the experiences in your DNA Code, differentiate between what suits you and what doesn't and then act in accordance with your conclusion; otherwise your insights have no value. Your mission is to differentiate and to act accordingly. Be careful, you have the tendency to cover things up.

A Third Sphere can often be recognised by inner peace, quiet observation, affability. These are often elusive people.

Third Spheres see both sides of the coin at the same time, in contrast to the Second Spheres. The latter can empathise with the other party, but they don't do this simultaneously, it takes them time and effort.

A Third Sphere does have this skill. This means that they see more and understand how things work more quickly.

This means that they have a different attitude to life. They can act from this knowledge, choosing whether or not to take others into account. The Third Sphere ultimately wants to elevate. They want to do good for themselves and others. They also offer their insights unconditionally.

Let's make it clear, Third Spheres aren't perfect and they also make mistakes to learn from. Elevating is a subtle game. The urge to convince others is ever present. Because they see more than others, they can also get frustrated because others need more time and can't see what is quite evident to them as a Third Sphere.

> **3rd Sphere: Differentiate for yourself by applying your DNA Code and try to help others while doing so. Offer others your insights so that these help everyone. Your mission is to elevate while offering your insights unconditionally. Be aware, you have the tendency to humiliate others.**

It's fascinating to know how Sphere Behaviour affects relationships and working with others. I could also explain this theme in the chapter Relationship Mission, but I've chosen to do it here. That's because it gives you a clearer picture of the importance of the Sphere Behaviour characteristic. Here we go.

The easiest people to get on with are Third Spheres. They see both sides of the coin and can see things in relative terms as a result. They don't worry as easily because of their insights. They comprehend situations better.

A Second Sphere finds a Third Sphere exciting, but they also make them a little nervous. The Third Sphere is a bit intangible and often knows better because of their broader view of the situation. The 2nd Sphere doesn't like that.

Second Spheres often have difficulties with First Spheres. They can't understand how people can't make choices for themselves, can't develop their own vision. They also only see one side of the coin and that is their own side. They can put themselves in others' shoes, but that takes effort.

Second Spheres feel best with other Second Spheres. First Spheres tends to hitch their wagon to a Second Sphere. This often gives the Second Sphere an uneasy feeling, as if someone is trying to rob them of their freedom.

So, you can argue that Sphere Behaviour leads to double insights, firstly about yourself but also about your relationship with others.

Does that make it better to have a relationship with someone with the same Sphere Behaviour? Maybe, but it's not necessarily so.

Already we can see that you need to be careful interpreting one single characteristic. Your DNA Code forms a whole and that whole fits or doesn't fit. You should never use just one characteristic to decide what fits best.

Ultimately, your feelings are a good judge. They give you the whole picture. You'll certainly find explanations in the DNA Code for possible obstacles in a relationship or when working together.

Learning to deal with this is another part of your growth in wisdom. It's essential that you allow others to be who they are. Acceptance is the basis for spirituality, accepting who you yourself are and who others are.

You might wonder if this division into Spheres isn't a kind of class structure, where one person is better than another. There is indeed that chance. However, every person is equally valuable, there's just a difference in the amount of wisdom which has been built up.

Personally, I have more sympathy for a First Sphere who is "real" than a "false" Third Sphere, for these do also exist. Your Sphere Behaviour tells you something about your wisdom level, but not about then acting according to your wisdom. That's the very definition of stupidity: knowing something and not applying it.

In essence, Sphere Behaviour teaches you the following things which are actually true for everyone:

Make a distinction for yourself between what suits you and what doesn't. This is true of both material objects as well as people:

> *Acting distinctively is the right way to walk your path.*

Act according to the insights you have gained:

> *It's good to know and to not forget.*

Let others be free to act, don't force them into anything and be selective in offering your wisdom:

> *Don't cast your pearls before swine if you want to thrive.*

Sphere Behaviour is the basis of your DNA Code, so bear it in mind. How does it work? Well, it's a matter of consciousness. You start by being unconscious and you don't know anything about your Sphere Behaviour. In that case it's also difficult to bear it in mind. That will only be possible if you listen closely to your intuition.

Once you become conscious, it requires an act of will to retain that consciousness. Obviously, that can't work all the time. However, by regularly paying attention to it, you can develop your skills, so that you can apply it in a superconscious way, without effort.

This is actually true of all your Soul Characteristics, you evolve from unconsciously incompetent, to consciously incompetent, to then becoming consciously competent and to end up as superconsciously competent.

Compare this to learning how to drive, you can do this on automatic pilot after a while. If you don't keep up your skill level, you'll soon experience the consequences. That's also how it works with Soul Characteristics.

To finish off this chapter, don't forget that others aren't in the same place on their path and that they have other characteristics. This leads to a beautiful variety of people and that makes the world a colourful place.

Accepting others is and will always be the basis for working together. Focus mainly on your own path, try not to change others, because it won't work anyway. Know that your environment will change with you if you change yourself. I'll come back to that later.

Basic Profile: Finders and Seekers

Your Basic Profile is a characteristic which you have chosen for this life and which determines your behaviour to an important extent. It explains the difficulties which you sometimes have interacting with one another. The division is simple, you are a Seeker or a Finder. I'd like to give you the main points about both characteristics.

A Finder is a straightforward person who goes for their goals and sees one clear way to get there. They don't explore any other possibilities and they require clarity. This allows them to act without asking many questions.

In contrast, a Seeker looks for possibilities and weighs up options. They get their kick not so much from achieving something as from finding out how to get there.

Seekers get on well with each other, with the possible trap that lots of things get explored and there's not a lot of action.

Finders don't understand all that "endless exploring" and want to act. Deeds not words, is their motto, aiming straight for their target, with no diversions.

> **Finder: Focuses on results to change the current situation, efforts need to result in personal advantage. Can be typified as the expert, wants to increase.**

> **Seeker: Focuses on pushing back limits, striving for insight and expansion, thinks ahead, has a vision. Can be typified as a generalist, wants to improve themselves.**

You might recognise this characteristic in yourself and others. It explains why you often don't understand one another.

There are other possible traps for relationships and working together contained in this characteristic. By taking each other into account, you can learn to deal with this shortcoming.

Seekers find Finders' attitudes demotivating. That's because a Finder only wants to work towards a result, not examine possibilities.

Seekers gain their fulfilment precisely from seeking. At work a Seeker often won't accept management from a Finder. Another effect of this characteristic is the sensitivity for remuneration. This works optimally for Finders, remuneration is a great motivator.

Seekers also like to receive good remuneration. However, they quickly see it as an entitlement, a normal thing, a self-explanatory appreciation which is to be expected. It won't motivate them. They won't work harder because of remuneration.

This characteristic also plays a significant role in relationships and then mainly when Seekers and Finders live together. The key to a relationship is then mutual acceptance.

Tackling simple matters is experienced completely differently by Seekers than Finders. This is a source of conflict and mainly misunderstanding. It may lead to a great deal of frustration. That's why it's essential to accept others as they are.

But what if you experience that accepting another is just a bridge too far? That you have really reached a boundary that you don't want to cross! The essential question in this case is: Does your partner (or your job) suit your Soul? You can find out how you can determine that later.

I'd like to mention, if you can't accept someone, draw your conclusions and leave. Don't live in frustration, it won't make you happy. Feel how far your boundaries go. Acceptance shouldn't become repression; the key lies in your feelings, because once again, that is the language of your Soul.

An important development should be stated about Finders. I'll come back to it in the Evolution Code, but I would like to mention that being a Finder is the only characteristic in the DNA Code which can change.

If you put in the required effort, then it is possible to evolve from a Finder to a Seeker. You can achieve this as a Finder, if you make a conscious choice and if you work on yourself.

It's a fact that the vast majority of conscious people who are interested in spirituality are Seekers. That fits the characteristic of seeking yourself.

How do you become a Seeker or a Finder? Well, when you incarnate from the Spirit World, your characteristics are set. One time you are a Finder, another time a Seeker. In that way, you can learn to deal with both characteristics. So, you can build on your wisdom from two positions and broaden your experiences.

I don't want to tell you much more about the Basic Profile here. Brief and to the point should be enough for now.

Types: Thinker, Doer, Feeler

The Types are a third part of your DNA Code. It's a very important characteristic which is easy to spot. It often explains your own actions and those of others. You could say that it's almost necessary to take this characteristic into account. This is not to prevent you getting into trouble, but so that you can understand others.

There are three Types, one of the Types will fit you.

> **Doer: Focuses on reality, looks for action and results, wants to create and make things happen in practise, using tangible concepts.**

> **Feeler: Senses situations quickly and finds emotions important, adds emotional elements to situations, is empathic, strives for harmonious collaboration.**

> **Thinker: Strives for knowledge and insights, goes looking for Why, needs communication and sparring partners, lets themselves be led by their thoughts.**

It's important to know that every Type, thinks, does and feels and that this should happen in this order. This is how the Type Circle is created.

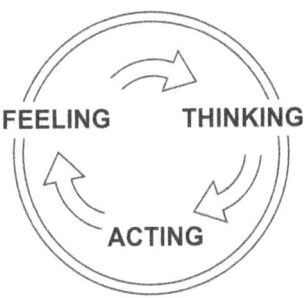

Working through the circle allows a total experience to take place. In that way, you really live through it and that's the basis for feeling properly and for gaining insights. That's why

33

applying the Types is so important.

So, the order with which you apply the Types is fixed, thinking – doing – feeling – thinking – doing – feeling... You automatically go around this circle several times per day.

Your own Type tells you where you start your own circle during an experience. This too is crucial. The Thinker starts by thinking, the Feeler with a feeling, the Doer with action.

A Feeler who firstly thinks without having felt, will almost always reach the wrong conclusion. This is true of all the Types.

The Type Circle is the basis for sentimental differentiation, an essential part of finding your Soul Path. So how does it work?

The most important principle in this circle is to start at your Type, until you feel something. From that point onwards, the following happens for each Type.

As soon as you have a feeling, the next step is to think about that feeling. This leads to a conclusion which is your prompt to action and doing. By doing something you arrive in a feeling. Call it a "final feeling".

If you have a pleasant feeling, then you've acted in the right way, if you have an unpleasant feeling, then you've reached the wrong conclusion.

Isn't it good that your feelings become a compass in this way? It seems obvious, but it often goes wrong. Thinking about your feelings is a difficult task for a lot of people. It requires a lot of practise and, mainly, being conscious.

Another frequent mistake is keeping yourself locked in thoughts, spending hours or nights chewing things over without finding a solution. The solution is simple, do something, because then you start feeling your emotions again and you can carry on. The circle itself will keep telling you what your next step should be.

Switching between feeling and thinking without acting is another possible trap, because in this way you'll also arrive at incorrect insights.

But I'd mainly like to stress that your Type determines the way in which you act. The Thinker wants to talk first and understand what something is about. A Feeler first wants to experience how it affects them and the Doer wants to turn their first impulses into deeds.

If you have no knowledge about your partners, children's or colleagues' Types, this can lead to misunderstandings. A Thinker doesn't understand why a Feeler needs some time before they can react and the Doer doesn't understand why the other Types don't take any immediate action.

Insight into each other's Types and accepting how others are, is also the basis for living together smoothly. Give the Feeler time to feel a situation fully and don't ask for a direct response. Let the Doer follow their first impulse, because that is how they learn how best to deal with the situation and let the Thinker talk about their ideas, because this gives them motivation.

This is a characteristic which we probably nearly all recognise. Unfortunately, not many allowances are made for it. Everyone assumes that others are just like them. They expect the same pattern, but that's not often the case. Friction can emerge as a result, which can grow into problems. Now that you know all this, you can also deal with it.

Know that by unveiling your Soul Path, you also learn to act in the same ways as the other Types. The combination of thinking, doing and feeling leads to a complete experience. Its conclusion can be added to your own knowledge or wisdom. This is how you shape your conscience.

You can consult your conscience, the sum of your experiences, in a future, similar situation. In this way, your conscience or intuition can immediately tell you how best to deal with it.

The key to yourself is feeling, that's the language of your Soul. So, learn to feel in the moment how something affects you. Think about what that feeling is telling you and let this conclusion determine your actions. That's how you keep finding your path.

If you find it difficult to feel, then ask yourself "what effect does this have on me, how do I feel?". If this doesn't work, start to talk about your experience. Your feeling will become clear through the act of talking.

Meditation

Let's take a quick detour. I'd like to talk about meditation in this chapter. This subject may not seem well placed, but nothing could be further from the truth, as you're soon to find out.

Meditation may conjure up an image of someone sitting crossed legged with their hands on their knees with their thumbs against their little fingers, trying to repress any thought in order to find peace. That's the Eastern image of meditation. But this may not be the right way of meditating for you.

Meditating means focusing on yourself and the Spirit World. It's a very individual thing, that everyone develops in their own way. Your Type plays an important role in this, which is the reason for this detour.

You mustn't underestimate the importance of meditation. I can only advise you to take your time to do so every day. It's an essential part of unveiling your Soul Path.

So, what do you actually do during meditation. You focus on your inner self, to gain insights, to let experiences sink in, to activate your consciousness, to find answers.

During meditation, breathe deeply towards your stomach and focus on your inner self. Close yourself off from external stimuli. The first step is become aware of your Soul. Your Soul is housed near your stomach, in your solar plexus.

So, following your gut feeling is listening to and acting in accordance with your Soul! Meditating is per definition putting yourself in the here and now, being aware of reality and keeping both feet on the ground.

Accepting reality is a condition for this, you often tend to doze off into fantasies, images, mental delusions. That's not part of meditation at all.

You might need your own space to meditate where you won't be disturbed, some quiet music in the background, a candle or incense might help too. This could create the atmosphere in which you can best get in touch with yourself. This isn't necessarily the case, however, as it all depends on your Type.

For Feelers, an atmospheric environment works best. For them meditation can be defined as resting without thoughts. Feelers need this to feel comfortable in their own skin.

The beautiful thing about mediation is that for Feelers issues can become clear and insights can be reached through peacefulness. After the necessary resting time, explanations appear from nowhere for the things that you were concerned about.

You can then quietly reflect on that as a Feeler. See it as completing the circle, resting is feeling, then a thought appears, which determines your actions.

For Doers meditating quietly doesn't work, although this is not a hard and fast rule and a Doer can gain some satisfaction from peace and quiet. The Type does determine your being, however.

For a Doer, the best way to meditate is to reflect while doing something. This could be during an action which you can carry out on automatic pilot, such as ironing or doing DIY.

While you're doing, you enter the right state of mind to reflect. Tens of thoughts appear spontaneously in this way. Things become clear to you in this way.

The Thinkers meditation is a reflective evaluation. Thinkers find it incredibly difficult to meditate from rest as the Feeler does and become frustrated as a result. This can only lead to one conclusion: meditation is not for me.

A Thinker is a Thinker, so their meditation starts from thoughts. Through this a sort of inner dialogue starts up, a conversation with yourself, where questions and answers lead you to the insights you need.

> **Meditation according to your Type:**
> **Doers: Being reflectively active**
> **Feelers: Resting without thinking**
> **Thinkers: Reflective evaluation**

There is still another important additional remark to be made about meditation. Make contact with the Spirit World while you are meditating. This is a conscious attitude, in which you open yourself up to connecting with your Guide.

I can't explain on paper how that works. You'll have to learn how to do itself yourself by trying things out. When you have worked out how to do it, then you'll have an extra means by which to reach the insights you require.

How will you know if you have a connection? Well, you'll experience it. A blissful expression on your face, a peaceful feeling inside, these are the signs which indicate that you're in connection. As soon as you experience it, your real meditation will start. Stay in this state for a quarter of an hour, that's more than enough.

You can then start a conversation with your Guide and make use of their knowledge. It's possible that if you conduct an inner dialogue, that you'll start to wonder where the answers are coming from. Am I not thinking this all up myself? Well, it isn't relevant who is thinking it up, whether it's coming from the Spirit World or from your own wisdom, it doesn't matter. We're all part of the Greater Oneness and so we are One.

Finally, practising meditation teaches you to be meditative. What should that mean to you? See it as an attitude to life, where you'll experience less and less unconscious moments, where you'll experience and pause at reality in full consciousness, more and more.

You'll automatically wonder, what am I feeling about this, why is this happening to me, what do I need to learn from this? That's how you'll learn to accept reality. Be careful, you can exaggerate this attitude by overthinking and that isn't meditative. It boils down to your intuition, your gut feeling and not your rational mind.

It takes some practise, but Rome wasn't built in a day.

Birth Code

So now we've finally arrived at the Number Codes. I explained Soul Growth in 21 steps in the introduction. Each step has a Number Code with its corresponding characteristics.

It's not easy to explain your Birth Code. The theory will only become transparent if you look at it from the perspective of experience. That will allow you to understand it all.

I can't explain everyone's Codes in detail here. That's why I'm giving you some theory which you will just have to work through. If you read through this with your own Code in mind it's bound to become easier to understand and if you have some experience with the Code, then it's quite comprehensible.

Your Birth Code consists of 4 number combinations, each one standing for one of the 21 steps mentioned earlier. Each of these characteristics contains specific attributes which determine your true self.

Each of these characteristics have a (+) and a (-) description. The positive side tells you how the Code is carried out properly. The negative side expresses an excess or a lack in the implementation of the characteristic.

You could see the (-) side of the characteristic as an incorrect interpretation, an excess or lack. Incorrect is a relative term, however: everyone makes mistakes and that's how it should be. That's part of your learning process. You can't learn without making mistakes.

By applying the excess as well as the lack, you get to know the extremes of your Code, which allows you to find the middle way. At least, it will if you are aware of your actions.

This makes your Code an especially useful manual. You get a point of reference against which you can weigh your actions and determine for yourself if you've found the right balance.

The extraordinary thing is that it's not a one-time event. You are looking to implement your true self in every situation and in every circumstance, so you could easily have 1000 aspects to your Code to get to know, so that will keep you busy for a while.

Now for some more explanation about the Code itself. Your Birth Code comes with some specific terms, Sphere Step, Stage Phase, Pitfall and Settler. The following example indicates how these work. Imagine that your Birth Code is 2.2/2.6 – 1.7/3.4. This means:

- Sphere Step 2.2, valuing possession and values: learn to use your Soul Feeling to deal with value and self-worth.
- Stage Phase 2.6, investigating: learn to investigate your Soul Feeling from every angle.
- Pitfall 1.7, giving up: learn to use your Soul Feeling to let go of what you don't believe in or trust.
- Settler 3.4, showing comprehension: learn to show comprehension according to your Soul Feeling.

Just as a reminder, the first number in 2.2, your Sphere Step, shows your Sphere Behaviour. You were born as a Second Sphere, I've already explained what that means.

The characteristics of your Birth Code determine your Soul Mission. In this life, you want to devote yourself to learning how to apply this Code. Your final aim is to completely master your Sphere Step.

Your Soul Mission is to get to know every nook and cranny of this characteristic. That determines your actions, the things which motivate you and what you need to feel good.

The Sphere Step is the most important number of all. It's the main theme running through your life. Stage Phase and Settler are talents which you develop, to implement your Sphere Step in an optimal way. This will become clear in the next chapter Age Code.

The implementation of your Code always has its own accents. That's why I'm only giving you a few sentences which describe each characteristic.

Look at how you act in concrete situations. Think about an example of when it worked well and when it went wrong.

Compare the general description of the characteristic with your own actions. In that way, you can find out how you implement your characteristic and you'll definitely find insights in yourself.

You gain experiences with every Code to find out what suits you. So, you're learning by doing; through consciously reflecting on your experiences and on your feelings, you gain clarity for yourself.

That isn't easy. Another's Code always seems simpler. You experience your own Code as the most difficult. That is partly because you have blurred vision from being up close to yourself. You can see someone else from a certain distance and that makes observation clearer. The trick is to apply this to yourself. Observe your own actions. Look at yourself in a neutral way and step outside yourself when doing so. This may sound a little odd, but it does work.

Maybe the following comparison will help. If you're sitting in your seat, then you can't do anything with your seat yourself, such as shifting it, cleaning it, turning it around or looking at it. As soon as you get up, you get a much better view of your seat and you can do something with it. So, to do that you have to get up out of your seat.

So, to get to know yourself better, the best idea is to step outside yourself. Then you'll get a better view and you'll become aware of what can be adjusted.

Let's get back to the Code. We'll go through it quickly. I'll give you some main themes for each Code which will give you an initial idea what this is all about. It's a good addition to the Codes which have been worked out for you later in the book. There you'll find the (+) and (-) side of each Code.

You might find that reading through all the Codes is a mountain of information, which is too high for you. You won't be able to work through all of these in one go anyway. See it as a reference book which you can use if you get stuck in your own Codes or if you'd like to get to know someone else's Code better.

I do still think it's important to make this overview, because it gives you an overall picture of the various characteristics and their mutual differences.

OVERVIEW NUMBER CODES:

1.1: Tackling: You learn how to tackle things, how to stick up for yourself. An act of will is needed to arrive at a result. So, don't just give up. The biggest mistake you can make is doing nothing. So, act even if you don't know for certain if it's the right approach. By tackling things, you can find out, because acting leads to feeling and feeling leads to insight.

1.2: Persevering: You learn to keep going in sticking up for yourself and in not giving up easily. You explore whether something really suits you by keeping going at it for long enough. The biggest mistake is becoming stranded in stubbornness or giving up too easily.

1.3: Daring To Confront Yourself And Others: You learn to confront yourself and others as well. This is necessary to defend your own interests. So, you stick up for yourself, if needs be, with powerful words and that may also be a confrontation with yourself - is my hard statement right? You'll find out through a process of confrontation. The biggest mistake you can make is avoiding confrontation, because you won't learn anything at all in that way.

1.4: Sowing And Growing (Multiplying): You learn to approach things with patience, to sow a seed, cherish it and give it the time to grow. You learn to appreciate that allowing things time leads to the best results. Impatience is your biggest mistake.

1.5: Daring To Make Mistakes: You learn to overcome your fear of making mistakes. You naturally tend to be hesitant, because you're expecting things to go wrong, but you can only really find out by trying. So, dare to take action. If it's wrong, then learn something from it. If it's good, then that's good too.

1.6: Experiencing Emotions: You learn to experience emotions, including fear. This requires a lot of courage. But know, that if you feel fear, you're doing well, because allowing your fear and emotions in makes them disappear so you can discover the essence. So, don't flee from your fears and don't deal with them too rationally.

1.7: Giving Up Of What Doesn't Suit You: You learn from your experiences what suits you and what doesn't. Again and again, you are confronted by the question: Can I trust this? Should I hold onto this or let it go? The key lies in keeping what can be trusted and letting go of everything else, both people as well as things.

2.1: Making Your Own Choices: You learn to make your own choices, stick up for what you yourself want. That won't work the first time, but through making choices, you'll ultimately arrive at your inner Soul Choice. You may possibly have to adjust your conclusion several times, until you feel that it is a real choice which suits you. Keep hold of it in that case and be consistent. Your biggest mistake is breaking this promise to yourself.

2.2: Valuing Possessions and Values: You learn by experience what's really valuable to you and in that way, you develop your own sense of self-worth. Your values scale is a personal, inner evaluation and you learn to act according to your conclusions. Your biggest mistake is looking for value outside yourself and letting it depend on things over which you have no control.

2.3: Differentiating Through Feelings: You learn to experience pleasant and unpleasant feelings to differentiate what you really want, what suits you. You also learn that unpleasant feelings are important and teach you things about yourself. So, learn to enjoy savouring pleasant and unpleasant feelings as well, and draw your conclusions from them.

2.4: Setting Boundaries: You learn by experience where your boundaries lie towards the outside world. So, say where your boundaries are and experience if these are right. If a boundary doesn't feel right, adjust it until you experience it matching your inner self. Watch over this boundary, that's the only way to deal with yourself respectfully. Your biggest mistake is allowing others to set your boundaries or wanting to determine boundaries for others.

2.5: Differentiating Major From Minor Matters: You learn what is really important to you and what isn't. By dropping the minor aspects (relinquishing) you'll feel good about yourself. Your biggest mistake is to relativize important matters.

2.6 Investigating: You learn to arrive at conclusions by investigating a situation from different angles. In that way, you can find the answers to what suits you. Use the combination of your actions, feelings and thoughts to do this. This will give you the right results. In this way, you'll learn to act in an increasingly more intuitive way and to retain what you have learned.

2.7: Letting Go The Urge To Impose: You learn that it's unnecessary to demand recognition to achieve results. So, you look for a wiser way of acting than forcing, without letting others walk all over you and while still sticking up for yourself. Feel that your urge to impose isn't actually a very useful approach and let it go.

3.1 Working Together: You learn that working together is an unconditional offer which others can accept or reject. You also learn to feel who you would like to work with and who not. If collaborating feels good, then you can elevate yourself and others to a higher level.

3.2: Sharing: You learn to share what you have experienced and you know, that this benefits you and may be of use to others. You learn when it makes sense to share things and when it doesn't. You learn this by pausing to reflect on your experiences and by drawing conclusions from them.

3.3: Developing Inner Balance: You learn to achieve inner balance between your male and female side, your thoughts and feelings. You also learn to do this in relation to others and you'd like, if possible, to raise yourself and others to a higher level. You're trying to go further than the earthly and the material in this way and you are searching for deeper levels and experiences.

3.4: Showing Comprehension: You learn to show comprehension for yourself and others by reflecting on your experiences. In this way, you can find out what you understand and what you don't. You want to show understanding to others and so, raise yourself and others to a higher level.

3.5: Elevating With Passion: You learn to act with passion and through your drive you can raise yourself and others up to a higher level. Through your experiences you find out where your passions lie and where they don't. This leads to insights which give focus to your actions.

3.6: Inner Knowing: You learn how to make use of your inner knowing, your intuition. By being loyal to this, it becomes clear to you what you really want and what you don't. You also want to offer your wisdom to others in this way, because by experiencing this you can develop your own wisdom and elevate others to a higher level.

3.7 Unconditional Surrender: You learn that applying conditions is superfluous and that loving actions can only work by not making any demands. You learn to surrender to the moment and to make maximum use of the moment, to elevate yourself and others to a higher level. You also learn to deal with your urges and to realise that these keep you from being who you really are.

Another way to look at the Code is to look at both numbers individually. This is because these also have their own meanings and splitting them often provides an extra angle.

So, you can learn in another way what your Code means for you and how you can best put it to use as well.

Each number has a (+) side, a correct implementation and a (-) side, an incorrect implementation, just like the complete Code.

The first number of your Code means:

1: (+) gathering (-) destroying

2: (+) distinguishing (-) covering up

3: (+) elevating (-) humiliating

The second number in your Code means:

1: (+) tackling (-) dawdling

2: (+) enriching (-) impoverishing

3: (+) warmth of feeling (-) coldness

4: (+) heartiness (-) heartless

5: (+) perfection (-) chaos

6: (+) intuition (-) normative

7: (+) trust (-) distrust

You can find a more extensive explanation further on in the book.

It's useful to know that you are striving to carry out the positive sides of the numbers and that you can make mistakes in one or both numbers.

This leads to a series of combinations. To return to the earlier example, imagine that you are 2.2, and carrying it out incorrectly: you might be covering things up, doing things which devalue you or devaluing yourself and covering it up.

Now that you have a picture of every Code, I'd like to add

the next step. Again, it's a lot to take in in one go, so you might have to chew on it for a while. So, make sure you feel whether you are ready for it.

Ready? Okay, here we go! Your Birth Code consists of 4 characteristics and these characteristics are mutually connected.

The strange thing is, as soon as you make a mistake in your Birth Code, and therefore, against your Soul, you'll drop down from one Code into another, without realising it and you'll almost certainly make an incorrect implementation of these characteristics.

This cascade of incorrect actions explains your own behavioural patterns. This teaches you to see how you are acting if you make a mistake against your Soul. This is an important facet in discovering your Soul Path. So, teach yourself how to see through yourself.

An incorrect action against your Soul always takes place in a concrete situation. If you want to learn something about yourself, then you'll need to do this in practice. The implementation of your Birth Code is therefore dependent on the situation you are in. You may act correctly at work and incorrectly in your relationship or vice versa.

Conclusion: never look at yourself generally, but always proceed from a real event. That makes spirituality very concrete. It's the only right way to look at yourself. An example might make this clear.

Imagine your Birth Code is 2.2/2.6 – 1.7/3.4, as stated in the previous example. Let's apply this to your work situation.

Imagine, you're acting against your Soul and make a mistake in your Sphere Step in your contact with your boss. An incorrect implementation could mean that you don't see the value of what is happening to you, you've let the value be stolen by another, you don't realise what is valuable to you or you deal badly with possession. These are just some of the possibilities.

Through your mistake in your Sphere Step, you also threaten to implement your Stage Phase incorrectly. It's a sort of blind spot, which you have ended up in unconsciously.

The consciousness of your Stage Phase can still help you to see through this, that you are not working in line with your true self. But it is more probable that unconsciously you're applying this Code incorrectly as well. In this example, this is 2.6. You may act in a normative way or approach a situation in a very one-sided manner. If you do subsequently succeed in implementing this characteristic well, you understand the situation and end up with both feet back on the ground. In other words, by using a correct 2.6, you can see your mistake in 2.2.

If that doesn't work, then you will end up in your Pitfall, the next number in your Birth Code. That is always connected to discomforts and disappointments. These show you that you aren't doing things correctly.

It's also difficult to see for yourself that you are in your Pitfall Behaviour. Your environment can make you aware of it and later you will be able to recognise it yourself. To see it for yourself, you'll need to create some distance, observe yourself, like a neutral observer of your own behaviour, as stated earlier.

Back to the example of 1.7: letting go. It's possible that you hold onto things which no longer suit you or that you give up too easily. Link this back to the concrete experience which you are having now. A theoretical or abstract analysis won't provide you with any insights.

If you experience disappointments, then it's safe to assume that you have wandered into your Pitfall. This is a sign which you can become aware of.

After implementing your Pitfall incorrectly, you arrive at your next characteristic, your Settler. The word should tell you enough, it can help you get out of your Pitfall. However, in the first instance, you'll also have the tendency to implement this characteristic in an incorrect way.

In this example, the Settler is 3.4, showing comprehension. You may well be showing understanding for others and not for yourself. You are being self-effacing for the general good.

You make this cascade of incorrect implementations again and again in your life, so that behavioural patterns develop around them. These can often be recognised as a combination of your Pitfall and Settler.

In this example, this is 1.7/3.4. You may show understanding for others and you no longer know how to differentiate what suits you and what doesn't, so you keep hold of the wrong things. This can also happen the other way around, you hold onto others, because you don't show yourself any understanding.

The combination of Pitfall and Settler gives you insights into your inauthentic behaviour. You develop tens of variations for yourself and don't realise that this isn't actually your real self.

I can only stress the importance of learning to understand your actions. With the DNA Code of your Soul you have the manual to get to know your authentic self.

It's a lot to digest, isn't it? I'm 'force-feeding' you right now, so I recommend you read this again slowly, step by step.

Every sentence is important. So, don't read over them too quickly, otherwise they won't have any impact. The next chunk is on its way, something else to chew on.

How can you stop doing all these incorrect implementations? Know that you actually get a chance to repair your mistake after every drop down into the next Code.

However, that isn't easy. Rome wasn't built in a day is the only correct motto here, so keep practising. Consciousness is an absolute pre-condition as well.

There are various possibilities to eventually break through the cascade of incorrect implementations and to return to your Sphere Step:

- Option 1: Split the numbers of your Settler. That's because, as stated, each 2-digit Code can be broken down into separate parts. Evaluating your situation from each of the relevant meanings often gives you the correct insights.

  In the example, that is 3 elevating and 4 heartfulness. The 3 tells you not to be self-effacing. That's because helping others by humiliating yourself is not the right way to act. The 4 points to your lack of heartfulness. You can find this out by asking yourself is my heart really in this or am I only doing this for someone else? Link this approach to your concrete experience. In that way, you'll arrive at the right insights.

- Option 2: Make use of the combined Code of your Settler. In this case that is 3.4, showing comprehension. Are you showing yourself enough comprehension for myself in this situation? If that doesn't help, link it to your first Code. In this example, that means, am I doing enough 3.4 for my 2.2. Or, in plain English, am I showing enough comprehension for what's valuable to me?

- Option 3: Apply your Stage Phase to this situation. In this example, that's 2.6. Investigate the event from various different angles. Know that you'll always apply your Stage Phase, whether consciously or unconsciously, to get out of your Pitfall.

I've already told you that the cascade of incorrect implementations is a long story. A practical example from your own life experience will make it all a lot clearer for you.

However, you often need some guidance from someone with knowledge about the DNA Code of the Soul to reach the right insights. As soon as you understand how it works, you can get to work by yourself.

I'd like to repeat that your Pitfall often leads to the greatest problems. You then encounter setbacks which point to you acting incorrectly. You can also stay stuck in your Pitfall for a long time, without being conscious of it, which leads to all kinds of consequences. I can only repeat the plea for consciousness.

Often this experience is linked to a victim role. Actually, this means that you are seeking the cause for what has happened to you outside yourself.

You see, you're never a victim. I'll come back to that in the coming chapters. You've always caused what happens to you. See it as a boomerang. If something happens to you, it's the return strike of a boomerang which you first threw yourself.

It's also fascinating to know that your Pitfall tells you which of the 21 Codes gave you the most difficulty in previous lives. You have got this Pitfall to pay extra attention to it and to experience both sides of it.

There are enhanced insights attached to each characteristic. In that way, you'll discover the increasingly deeper and finer layers of how you implement your true self. For example, when you're 60 you act differently to when you were 45. Nevertheless, you are still learning to implement the same characteristic.

The consequence of your gained wisdom is that your path becomes a little narrower. You now know part of your path and you know how best to act. That makes your path narrower and you can fall off it more quickly. This leads you to new insights. Call it enhanced insights, a never-ending story.

But know that applying your Code properly gives a feeling of satisfaction. Your Soul strives for this experience. This is how you create Heaven on Earth - by being who you are and by acting in line with your Soul Characteristics.

Making mistakes leads to unpleasant feelings. Putting these feelings into words often clarifies what you are experiencing and leads to correct insights. Feelings are, of course, the language of your Soul.

To be completely clear about this, your Heaven on Earth consists of both pleasant as well as unpleasant feelings and both can lead to satisfaction.

There are a lot of misunderstandings about this. Often people try to escape from unpleasant experiences, but this is also part of your path. Putting your feelings into words liberates you. Use this as your motto when traversing your Soul Path. Feeling is the language of your Soul. As the saying goes: He who doesn't want to feel, will burn their fingers.

The ultimate aim of implementing your Birth Code is gaining insights and acting accordingly. As you get to know yourself better, you'll understand how it works.

Don't forget to include your Sphere Behaviour in your Code. Gather, differentiate or elevate yourself or others. Here again, there are invariably insights involved.

This, in a nutshell, is your Birth Code. It's a mass of information which supports you when unveiling your Soul Path. When you have figured out how it works, you'll understand a lot more about your personal problems and you'll have tools with which to gain insights into yourself.

Age Code

There is an important extra remark needed about your Birth Code. There is a chronology in the application of your Code, depending on your age. The term Age Code is therefore self-explanatory: it explains how your Soul Path is unveiled throughout your life.

As a child, you are working on applying your Settler. To be completely clear, your Soul wants to get to know the positive sides of this characteristic. Through experience you learn how this characteristic works for you and it develops as your first talent. This talent becomes useful later to get out of your Pitfall as explained in the previous paragraph.

From 12 years old onwards, you turn towards your Pitfall characteristic. It's remarkable that as a teenager you want to experience both the positive as negative side of this. This explains the sometimes-difficult behaviour that teenagers show and how tricky it can be to grasp. Today something is white and tomorrow it's black. But that fits exactly with what the Soul wants to experience. This experience is needed so that a teenager can explore the boundaries of what is acceptable. This is how they develop their own frame of reference. They need this to learn to function independently in our society.

Parents find this difficult and do everything they can to keep their child on the tracks. This can have pernicious consequences for a child. This is because if a child doesn't develop their own frame of reference, life will become even more difficult.

Between 18 and 36 years old, you develop your Stage Phase as a talent, that's to say the positive side of this characteristic.

From 36 onwards, your focus is solidly on your Sphere Step. This is, as stated previously, your final aim, your Soul Mission.

> **Age Code:**
> - 0/12: Positive implementation **Settler**
> - 12/18: Positive and negative implementation **Pitfall**
> - 18/36: Positive implementation **Stage Phase**
> - 36+: Positive implementation **Sphere Step**

The Age Code explains why people change and their life visions develop and modify. This can be the basis for new life choices. Specific ages, such as 18 and 36, are often turning points, at least for those who live their lives consciously. I'll come back to this later.

And what if you don't succeed in implementing your Code? Does that have any consequences? It's important to know that you can't always carry out your Code correctly and that you learn precisely from making mistakes.

It's enough to implement your Code well in one single domain. If, for example, you don't succeed in carrying out your Code at home, but you do do so at school or in a youth group, then that's fine.

If you don't succeed in any domain, then it's a matter of refusal. You yourself are the source of this. Your Z-Code gives you insights into this, which I'll discuss in the next chapter.

I would still like to tell you the consequences of implementing the Age Code incorrectly. If you don't manage to carry out the right side as a child, teenager or young adult, then you'll have missed out on several life insights.

This means that you'll experience a number of setbacks from 36 onwards. These give you a new chance to reach insights. Often people see these setbacks as a punishment from God.

This is partly correct if you realise that you yourself are a speck of God. So, you cause these setbacks yourself and the incorrect reaction is then to seek the cause outside yourself.

You are always cause and effect. Everything that happens is the consequence of your own actions and the basis for learning life lessons. This gives you a totally different image of what happens to you. A setback is an opportunity. It just depends on how you look at it!

As a teenager, you need to implement both sides of your Code. If you only do the positive side and not the negative, you'll end up in the scenario described above. You'll run into setbacks after you turn 36.

If you only work on the negative side of your Code as a teenager, then that has a much greater impact. You'll develop a very negative attitude, you'll rebel against everything and everybody, you'll become morbid. This may lead to addictions, alcohol, drugs, attempts to escape from society. Because of your negative attitude, you'll also attract negativity. Birds of a feather flock together. The question is: which group do you want to belong to?

Still, I'd like to warn you against premature conclusions. Often people are too quick to state that they haven't succeeded in implementing their Code. Then you may have a distorted image of what is possible. So, don't judge too quickly, but be realistic. If you can't solve this, ask someone with the right knowledge for some advice.

I've already commented on how you can drop down from the one Code into another after incorrect implementations. Your age determines in which Code the cascade starts. If you're under 36, for example, then your Sphere Step hasn't come into play yet. First you act against your Stage Phase, then you drop down into your Pitfall and you do your Settler incorrectly as well. Conclusion: you can't make any error in a Code for which you haven't yet achieved the relevant age.

To complete the story about the Age Code, it's useful to know that your Sphere Step is the main theme running through your life. This seems contradictory but it isn't. As a child, teenager or young adult, you're carrying out your Age Code and practising your Sphere Step at an unconscious level.

When you turn 36, you've therefore already gained unconscious experience with this Sphere Step and you're then immediately able to implement it in the correct way. At least, you can if you've implemented your Age Code in the right way.

So, this has shown you how your Birth Code and Age Code work. It's allowed you to cognitively understand how it all fits together. But being able to deal with your Code with your feelings is at least as important.

To fully take on an insight, you need to live through it fully. That's how you absorb it. Without feelings, this isn't possible, then you'll quickly forget your conclusion. By feeling, you can turn your experience into knowing. Your knowing, conscience and wisdom are the basis for how to act another time.

Ultimately, it's all about acting, that's real spirituality, growing in wisdom and in your ability to apply your life lessons. Step by step you'll learn the facets of your Code. Acting in accordance with yourself ultimately gives you contentment.

If you don't do this, your life will become exhausting, you'll become demotivated. We often seek the cause for this outside ourselves, but this only indicates that you are not living in accordance with your own authentic self. See this again as a sign from your Soul, asking for adjustments.

Those who live life consciously use these signs to look at themselves in the mirror, to confront themselves and to search for insights. In this way, their Soul Path is unveiled and they'll receive clarity about life.

Well, you might need to take a breather now. You've already tackled the toughest part of the book. What follows is easier to grasp intuitively, even if I'm going to dig further into your path.

Knowing what you already do, you are certain to already be able to tackle a lot of things. Hopefully, you'll be able to keep up the confrontation with yourself. Once the seed has been planted, growth can no longer be stopped. You'll learn that by trial and error. In that way, you can discover your emotions and fears and you'll learn to hold onto what you can trust.

Know that this is a conscious choice, one which will only increase your sense of self-worth. Feel, set boundaries, determine what is really important to you. Do this from every angle, learn to reduce your urge to impose.

You may want to start working with this with others and share what you have already experienced yourself. That's how your inner balance will emerge, by developing your understanding of yourself and others. It'll ignite the passion in you, so that your knowing will keep on increasing and you can unconditionally surrender to what you really want, your Soul's Will.

Contact with others is essential to do this. The Relationship Code in the next chapter is the roadmap for this.

RELATIONSHIP MISSION

Relationship Mission, what is that? Well, your Soul learns from individual experiences, the characteristics for this are mainly in your Birth Code. Your Soul also learns from contact with others and there is a series of other Codes which is important for that.

These have been brought together under the term Relationship Mission. See it as a series of characteristics which teach you to live with others in line with your authentic self, to your Soul. You can gain a lot of wisdom from this as well.

The Relationship Mission contains the following characteristics:

- Mars or Venus Code
- Q-Code
- Z-Code
- Sphere Fear

If you want to work on these Codes, make sure that you have some insights into your Birth Code beforehand. This is level two and if you haven't worked through level one, it doesn't make much sense to start with this.

I do need to mention that there are aspects in your Birth Code to do with how you interact with others. The Sphere Behaviour, the Basic Profile and the Type certainly fall into this category.

I already explained this in the previous chapter, because it gives you additional insights into the characteristic, which makes it easier to understand. But actually, the impact of the characteristic on living with others belongs in this chapter. That's why I'm repeating the main points.

Sphere Behaviour: A Third Sphere can get on with everyone. A Second Sphere finds the dependency of a First Sphere difficult and finds a Third Sphere difficult to fathom, which they find unpleasant. A First Sphere is more than happy to follow a Second Sphere, but the latter doesn't like that.

Basic Profile: A Finder wants to go straight for their target and is looking for personal advantages on the way. A Seeker finds their motivation in laying out their options and exploring which best suits them. A Seeker can become demotivated by a Finder approach.

Type: A Thinker and a Feeler work best together. They complement and strengthen each other if they allow enough space for the other's characteristics. Two Feelers can end up becoming enmeshed in endless feeling. Two Thinkers can philosophise endlessly and not take any action. Two Doers go into action together without a plan and can lose each other on the way.

Again, I'd like to underline that these shortcomings can be overcome by accepting others as they are and allowing for the others personality. If that is a bridge too far for you, then you should draw your conclusions.

So, this short recapitulation is sufficient for the introduction. Let me go into the other Relationship Codes one by one in more depth now. It's an illuminating story with a lot of new aspects to it.

Mars & Venus Code

The most important of all the Relationship Codes is your Mars or Venus Code. Next to your Birth Code, it's what gives you the most difficulties in life. Venus or Mars indicate how you influence the outside world and how you're influenced by the outside world.

Of all the new aspects in this book, this is by far the most revelatory. Don't underestimate this account, for if you choose to work with it, you'll be entering a confrontation with yourself and your environment. That will change your world fundamentally; to be clear, this will be a good thing. See it as a cornerstone of the unveiling of your Soul Path.

You might wonder why this has only just been mentioned and not earlier. Well, when the time is ripe, I pass on what is manageable. If I'd given you all the information at once, that would have been an indigestible amount. That's why I've done so step by step. I do however want to explain everything in this book. That makes it tough and a lot to chew on, but it's good to bundle the collection of all of this into one whole. It's up to you to deal with it wisely. So, don't choke on it!

Let me explain what this is about. Everyone is a Mars or a Venus. This has nothing to do with being a man or woman. So, saying that men come from Mars and women from Venus is just a quip. It is true that there are specific male and female characteristics. But that's another story, which I don't want to go into now.

Until now, the Mars and Venus characteristic was known as an astrological aspect, only applying to a limited number of people. What's new is that everyone has something to do with this.

Astrologically, you call this characteristic Mars and Venus Retro, because you've established that people born in the retrograde period of these planets have specific characteristics.

That's all true. Astrology is another way to explain the

Message that I want to communicate here. You just need the correct astrological approach to find the right connections. Unfortunately, I've ascertained that there's been some fiddling going on in this area, but that's not the matter at hand now.

Back to the Mars Venus story. Each of us encounters this characteristic. The reason why I definitely want to explain this is that more and more people are working through their last life in the material world.

The group of conscious people who are seeking insight is increasing and the speed with which the number is growing has led to them evolving past the Third Sphere. I'll explain this matter in the chapter about the Evolution Code.

For now, know that when you evolve past the Third Sphere, that your Soul no longer needs the material to further unveil its Soul Path. Then you stop incarnating, you do your further Soul Growth in the Spirit World.

This fast growth of many has a side effect. Learning to deal with your Mars or Venus characteristic, depends on contact with the physical. It isn't there in the Spirit World. If you're in your last life on earth, then it's important to master this characteristic.

The sooner you start, the better. The longer you wait before tackling it, the deeper your Mars or Venus habits will be engrained in your Soul and the more difficult it'll be to change anything about it.

To be clear, I can only advise you to get to work with your Mars or Venus, you will fare well by doing so.

Know that tackling this characteristic is a Soul Mission for a Mars or Venus Retro. You experience this from birth.

It's advisable for a normal Mars or Venus to get to work with this characteristic. Know that this characteristic can get you into a lot of difficulties at an unconscious level.

What does that "get to work" entail? Well, this characteristic determines your interaction with others at an unconscious level. This interaction often works against your Soul, but you're not aware of that. So, it distracts you from your real self. That's a good reason to tackle this characteristic.

Working with your Mars or Venus is the process of becoming aware of your unconscious behavioural patterns towards others. You can only change what you acknowledge.

You might experience a form of withdrawal from others, reticence, introversion. Or maybe you have more of the feeling that others don't understand you, can't follow your ideas, that you don't get any recognition and that you can't find where you belong. These are both features of Venus and Mars.

The most important thing is that if you're aware of this, you can also change it within yourself. This can only have advantages. Let this argument prevail.

If you set to work with this characteristic, then you're doing that because it will give you a personal advantage – you'll be learning how to deal with others in a smoother way. Do you need any more motivation?

So, onto the next question. How does Mars or Venus come into being? Well, do you remember the introduction? Once upon a time there was a Big Bang when the Greater Whole, the Oneness, was split up into particles, Souls. At the moment the bang took place, this was a dramatic experience for the Souls.

Even if the Big Bang was a choice by the Greater Oneness and therefore by every Soul, the event didn't take place without any issues. Half was angry about going through it, the other half was sad that they'd have to be alone from now on. That is the basis of your Mars or Venus characteristic.

So, you start your Soul Path as a fledgling Soul. I've already gone into how you go through evolution. There are 21 wisdom levels to go through and you take another couple of steps in each life.

You start with ballast: one half is angry, the other half sad. Because you haven't been able to feel this emotion fully, put it into words or draw insights from it, this causes difficulties from the start.

That's why Marses encounter coincidences in which they can experience their anger, so that they can work through this load. Venuses get the chance to solve their sadness. I'll discuss how you can resolve Karma later. Between brackets, when I say Karma I mean the leftover ballast from unprocessed feelings which you lug around, from this and previous lives.

But first let me complete the Mars and Venus story. Your first lives see your ballast increasing, because feeling and putting your feelings into words isn't working well enough. Then, at a certain point in your evolution, the dam bursts when you experience a sufficiently traumatic experience that it marks you for all your subsequent lives.

This experience takes place somewhere in your First Sphere. This event is so extreme, that the Evolution Code which you have at that moment, stays with you in all the lives which follow.

This is when a new part of your DNA Code comes into being. From then on, your Mars or Venus characteristic is represented by 2 numbers: a Mars-Venus Pitfall and a Mars-Venus Settler.

Let me give you an example. Imagine you're a Venus and at the time of your traumatic experience your Evolution Code was 1.6/2.5. Then you'll carry this 1.6 (experiencing emotions) and 2.5 (differentiating between major and minor matters) with you in all your future lives.

This is the only part of your DNA Code which is constant for all your lives. All the other parts change over time, but only your Mars or Venus Code stays unchanged. That explains the great impact of this characteristic.

You need to know that at the moment of your traumatic event, you effectively experience a trauma and decide something like: I never want to go through that again.

You learn to protect yourself against those kinds of incidents. However, you do so in a completely incorrect way. You look for the path of least resistance and flee into the (-) sides of your Mars or Venus Code. You experience this as safe. However, you're not acting according to your Soul and then you build up more Karma!

It's a difficult story, which you'll have to turn around at some point. You are best off doing this in the material world. All the elements you need are available there, namely other people.

It's less logical to do this in the Spirit World; working through this characteristic is then very troublesome and takes many times longer. So, that's a good reason to get to grips with it.

You might wonder: why do we need to experience all of this? Your Mars or Venus ensures a lot of doom and gloom as you'll find out. Is it a punishment from God or a sort of fall from grace, which came into being when the gates to the Garden of Eden were closed?

Well, let's leave the fables to the fables and limit ourselves to the essence. Your Mars or Venus is solely a way to grow in wisdom. It's a derivative of the Original Wish of the Greater Oneness, as I explained in the introduction. Your Soul, the speck of God in yourself, wants to contribute to that.

How do you experience this characteristic? Before I explain that to you, you need to be warned. You're definitely going to have an automatic reaction to want to estimate whether you are one or the other. But then your rational mind has sprung into action, because you're not who you would like to be in your ideal world. So, don't make the mistake of continuing with your own assumption.

I'd especially like to warn you about the meaning of the words which I'm using. A Mars will interpret words differently to a Venus. That's a little strange, but further on I'll give you some examples which will make this clearer.

Again, I repeat, accepting who you really are is the basis for a spiritual life. The only way to get certainty about your DNA Code is to request it. There's no other way.

So, back to the question: how do you experience your Mars or Venus characteristic? Well, Marses feel misused, Venuses feel mistreated.

Marses often experience coincidences in which they experience being used, a the misuse of power. This is actually so they can solve their anger, from the Big Bang, if you recall. But unfortunately, they're not so good at feeling this anger.

The result is that Mars ignores this unpleasant feeling and turns anger into jealousy and envy. This is a typical human process. An unpleasant feeling which hasn't been felt fully or put into words, will express itself in one way or another. The unpleasantness is locked into your Being and tries to find a different form in which to escape.

For Mars that is jealousy and envy and this can even develop into schadenfreude, depending on the extent of the anger. These happen to be characteristics which are socially unacceptable. So, there's a good chance that you will repress them.

Venuses encounter coincidences in which they experience mistreatment. This mistreatment has a specific character. They experience this as an act of lovelessness, a form of psychological abuse. This makes the Venus very sad. Unfortunately, this feeling is also often avoided.

The Venus translates their sadness into aloofness and fatalism. This is often incomprehensible behaviour for their environment. Venuses will quickly get the reaction: Get over it. This makes you feel even less understood, you experience even more lovelessness and you delve deeper into your distancing and fatalism.

These processes are difficult to break through for both Marses as well as Venuses. The impact can sometimes last for days, weeks or months. So, this characteristic can determine your life to a very great extent.

The trigger for the misuse of power or the mistreatment is always a stimulus outside you. Becoming aware of this is part of learning to deal with this characteristic. That's why this Code belongs in the chapter on Relationships. It's the most important Code which causes difficulties in your dealings with others.

So, you experience the influence of the outside world and you have cultivated unconscious reflexes to deal with it. The external stimulus may be something tiny, a word, the tone in which something is said, a door which is slammed too hard, posture or just the way in which somebody approaches you.

The closer someone is to you, the greater the impact. People who mean nothing to you, don't affect you. But if the trigger comes from your partner, or from your parents or children, or from your best friend, then it hits home hard.

You can learn to see through external stimuli if you realise that you can learn to guard against them by adapting your own behaviour. Your Code gives you clues how to do this. It is a very personal story and learning to deal with it may require personal guidance.

You can also learn a lot from others and a group learning process is a good idea. That's because your reactive patterns are unconscious processes. You can't adjust anything that is unconscious; you don't even know they exist.

Becoming conscious is stimulated to a large extent by recognising a behavioural pattern in others. That should ring a bell about yourself. You become aware that you have also developed a similar pattern. Realising that is the starting point for change.

Allow me to delve deeper into the different characteristics and start by dissecting Mars.

A Mars is focused on the exterior world. That makes them very happy, even carefree about themselves. If something happens to them, then it's someone else's fault. They'll only rarely have the reflex that they're the cause of something. They forget, having designated something as being exterior, to look at themselves. You're still always both cause and effect of what happens to you.

In addition, Mars lives using tunnel vision. They want things to work as they want them to. Everything which lies beyond that they view as non-existent. This is how they can ignore, cover up, distort and manipulate parts of reality. This seems like bad will, but it isn't. Mars simply doesn't see that there's a reality beyond their tunnel. This behaviour bubble can be burst.

Because Mars wants things to go how they want, they have the tendency to do anything to get their own way. One result is a double agenda and exercising power on their environment is a very normal thing for them to do as well.

They appear to pay no attention to their environment when doing so. That's correct. Their behaviour often appears selfish. That's not how Mars experiences it, however. They're only aiming at what they believe in. They believe that they've got the right end of the stick and they want others to acknowledge that. They don't understand that others don't see that, which makes communication even more difficult.

Because Marses don't shy away from abusing power, they're very sensitive to that. To protect themselves and to reach their own goals, Marses have developed typical behaviours. The urge to get their own way is very great. They want to be the boss.

A first pattern emerges when Mars is afraid that they won't be able to force their point, then they go on the defensive. Defence is the result of not accepting what is. Reality doesn't fit their image. By going on the defensive, Mars hopes to be able to get their way in the end.

If this strategy doesn't work, they give up and behave like a victim. This can be expressed as not speaking, showing their displeasure non-verbally or withdrawing.

A second typical Mars-pattern emerges when they ascertain: I can do this, I'm going to fight for this! They want to pay back the feeling of being used in kind. The Mars then thinks in terms of hierarchies. This gives them a feeling of certainty about their position. If they don't know their position, they're difficult to handle.

This is an important realisation. Mars views everything in ranks. They tend to be uncertain by nature and by applying a ranking, they can overcome their uncertainty.

The main lesson which Mars has to learn is that a thing called equality exists and that hierarchy is only a means to function well in the material world in a certain situation.

Equality is the complete opposite to their hierarchical way of thinking. They have a lot of lessons to learn in this area. To do this they need a lot of experiences to go through consciously, so that they can extract the required insights from them. In that way, they learn that equality is the correct basis and they experience that in practise there are varying roles. One time one person is in the lead, another time it's someone else. This is how they can let go of their striving to always be right.

In addition, the Mars develops two talents, caring and curiosity. The last is a result of their focus on the outside world.

You could say that Mars can't do without the outside world, because then their frame of reference has gone. That's because everything is compared, because that leads to a hierarchy which gives them certainty.

Again, comparison often leads to disastrous consequences. Jealousy and envy can emerge, because they may conclude that others have something that they don't. If the Marses were to dig deeper into themselves, then they would find out that they don't want what the other has.

Unfortunately, all too often, they miss out this step and they fall back into the same trap. They need to learn that comparisons lead them further away from what they really want.

If you cluster all of Mars' characteristics, they seem like very unkind people. Especially if you're a Mars, then you might well have difficulties with this. But know that there is no good and no bad. Everyone is the same after all.

Now enough about Mars, let me discuss Venus. Venuses are focussed on themselves and only ever look for the cause of what happens to them within themselves. They often don't see an external stimulus which is causing everything which is happening to them.

Of itself, it's a correct conclusion to keep reflecting on oneself. However, Venus takes it too much to heart for things that aren't part of them. They have to learn to differentiate between what is up to them and what isn't.

In contrast to Mars, Venus doesn't have tunnel vision but a very open view. They try to take everything and everybody into account. You could say that their visor is opened far too wide, the complete opposite to tunnel vision. They have to learn to aim at only that which is important to them.

If they don't do that, this can have disastrous consequences. They'll quickly feel like a little, lost lamb, the victim of their goodness. They don't understand at all why the outside world doesn't see how hard they're trying to take everything and everyone into account. They don't realise that they're the victim of their own actions.

This is how Venuses act. They continually observe everyone and everything. They try to take all these stimuli into account in their behaviour. That's because Venuses mainly "want to be loved". The more they size up their environment, the greater the chance that they'll be accepted.

But that's where the shoe rubs; it's impossible to take everything and everybody into account. How does Venus know if their estimates are correct? They make it all hopelessly complicated for themselves and then becomes the victim of this.

When Venuses feel like a little, lost lamb, the victim of their own goodness, they have the tendency to retreat into virtual reality. They do this to protect themselves from influences from the outside world. That's logical. That's because in the outside world, they only ever encounter a lack of understanding. So, they often feel unhappy, become numb, feel powerless and then sad and lonely.

Their environment doesn't understand any of this, because on the outside there is often no trigger for this behaviour. Due to the lack of understanding, Venus only withdraws further. They have the tendency to hold themselves in. They don't see any solution for dealing with the world.

Actually, Venus is asking for recognition, look at me, please take me into account, love me! If that doesn't happen, then they'll become very insecure which leads to a lot of self-doubt. Their own sense of self-worth is then hammered into the ground. Furthermore, their plea for help is seldom answered.

The fact that Venuses want their environment to take them into account is a logical consequence of their own attitude. They expect others to act in the same way as they act. In their opinion, because they're taking everyone into account, they expect others to take them into account too. But essentially the cry for recognition is a form of power, because they expect something from their environment, and that isn't right.

This incorrect expectation is the result of a deeply rooted feeling of equality. They experience it as unfair that others don't take them into account. What they don't see, however, is that they've gone wrong by taking everyone and everything too much into account.

Venus' typical pattern is holding in. They are self-effacing, placing themselves in the background and running around in circles for others. That's better than maybe getting a rude awakening. However, because of that, they lose themselves. They pay the price for their behaviour.

The running around in circles for their environment which Venus does has its limits. At a given moment, enough is enough and the tiniest next happening will be the last straw. Then the bomb explodes. Venus feels kicked in their Soul and will finally start to stick up for themselves. Their attitude is, enough is enough.

That's quite a shock to their environment. It might be a tiny thing which causes the camel's back to break. For other, it seems like their behaviour is completely out of proportion. They don't realise how many straws of giving went before this last one.

This leads to misunderstanding, miscommunication, frustration and irritations. Talking is the only solution to this. Without talking, breaks can occur.

In general, Venus carries the consequences of their experiences of lovelessness. That's why they are often shy to make contact. They naturally distrust others and are afraid of being disappointed again.

That's why they hesitate to be vulnerable, to start a conversation. They are reining themselves in beforehand. This appears very reserved.

Ultimately, Venuses strive for equality but must learn to love themselves first. Each time they get a rude awakening, they are thrown back on themselves. In this way, they learn bit by bit to accept that they are who they are and they learn to adjust their behaviour.

As soon as they become aware that they are taking others too much into account, and are actually being very unloving towards themselves, they'll be able to change.

In this way Venus learns to be caring and wise with their environment and knows that they can use their strong ability to empathise to their advantage.

So, that's enough about Venus. It may be very confrontational to go through these characteristics and you may be wondering which you belong to. Often the initial reaction is that one recognises oneself in both, but know that you are either Mars or Venus.

I've already told you that the meaning which the Marses and Venuses give to one and the same word, can vary enormously. That's why it seems as if you're one or the other, but you never know for certain. That's why I'm going to give you some examples.

For Mars, being rejected means: I'm not getting my way; for Venus: I'm not good enough. For Mars, insecurity is: I don't understand the hierarchy and don't know my place; for Venus: there is inequality at work here and no-one is making any allowances for me. For Mars, making allowances mean: how can I get the other person to carry out my idea; for Venus: that they are respected, because their opinion is being taken into account.

The communication between Marses and Venuses is often unclear because of this confusion about each other's languages. They use the same words with different meanings, so this can lead to a lot of confusion.

Because of this confusion it is very difficult to work out for yourself which you are. You'll recognise words which are linked to one kind as a personal characteristic, but you may feel the meaning incorrectly. So once again, please be careful about reaching conclusions too quickly.

How can you learn how to deal with the Mars and Venus characteristics? Well, as stated before, some guidance could be useful to turn your unconsciousness into consciousness. But if you were to ask for your Code and knew which you were, then everything would start with accepting who you are.

If you don't accept that, then no consciousness will arrive and you'll be putting your head in the sand. That's possible and permissible; there is free will, after all. You and only you can take the decision to start working on yourself. Know, however, that sooner or later you'll take the step to tackle this.

After acceptance, it's important to gain insights into your behavioural patterns, linked to your Code. Again, external guidance is strongly advised. Let me explain the behavioural patterns in an example.

Imagine your Mars and Venus Code is 1.6 – 2.5. The behavioural pattern which you have developed to protect yourself against the outside world, is a combination of the incorrect implementation of both figures.

1.6 (-) can mean escapism or normative behaviour, 2.5 (-) can mean focussing on details or being too perfectionistic.

The combination could be: I'm focussing on details in a normative way or I'm going to try to prove myself by covering up my mistakes as well as possible or I downplay my emotions and shut off my feelings.

These are just examples, but know that you have developed tens of varieties depending on the situation. Often expressions which are typical to you can be related to this. You're not aware of any of this, so there's work to be done.

The next step in dealing with Mars or Venus is recognising and acknowledging the feelings which belong to each kind. Feeling and putting feelings into words is liberating. You need to learn how to deal with jealousy, envy and anger as a Mars and aloofness, fatalism and sadness as a Venus.

Once you have got this sorted out, you can learn to prevent yourself from dropping down into your Pitfall, by seeing through the external stimulus, and you can learn to implement your own Code well. If you are already in your Pitfall, then the right application of your Code can help you climb out of it again.

There are several tricks available, linked to the Code, but it's going too far to go into detail here. Even if there is a general rule for this, it needs to be worked out personally with guidance.

So, the main thing to remember is that Mars and Venus have an especially great impact on you and that you can learn to deal with this differently. If you do that, your world will change fundamentally.

There are two possibilities. Either you undergo external stimuli which means you get off track and you're unable to act according to your true self, or you become aware of these processes and learn to deal with them, which means that you stay yourself.

There's no better example of how you can take hold of your own destiny and shape your own life. You determine how the chips fall. See the first chip as an external stimulus. You don't have any control over that, but you do over the following chips. The key lies in your consciousness.

You develop your consciousness in two phases. The first step is learning how to deal with yourself. When you've mastered that, then you can focus on others. Knowing how things work with you goes a long way to helping you improve your life. It teaches you to increasingly be yourself.

Ultimately, a relationship is about two parties, where one stimulus prompts another. See it as a snowball effect which quickly turns into an avalanche.

It's important to know that the interaction between two Marses works completely differently than between two Venuses. There are different obstacles again between a Mars and a Venus. Yet again everything depends on completely accepting the other as they are.

When Marses are together they can fall into the trap of ending up in a power struggle. When Venuses are together they threaten to get stuck in their pathos. Every element is present for heavy confrontations between a Mars and a Venus; these may just teach them most of all.

So, the Mars and Venus business is a lot to take on! Does it make sense to you? I'd like to give you some advice.

The key is showing comprehension for yourself and others. Showing comprehension is a big challenge. The most difficult form is showing comprehension for someone who doesn't comprehend you!

Add the following elements to showing comprehension: communication, acceptance, tolerance and respect. I could write a whole chapter about each of these, but for now this will have to do. Searching for insights, working on yourself, letting the other be as he or she is, that's the motto.

You can only be who you are and develop your consciousness from there. Know that you change your environment by changing yourself. That's because your environment can indirectly feel a change in you, which changes them as well.

Enough about Venus and Mars, it's a whole story which will need to sink in. But we're not done yet, there are other Relationship Codes to go.

Q-Code

The Q-Code is the second typical characteristic of your Soul which determines your attitude to others. It gives your preferred position in a group and this characteristic also has a determining effect on your relationships. It explains your attitudes to others. It's an extra part of your Soul Characteristics, the impact of which shouldn't be underestimated.

The name is derived from quadrants. These are divided into two criteria, actives versus passives and leaders versus followers.

In this way you get 4 groups, each with its own characteristics. Just like the Sphere Behaviour, this characteristic tells you something about yourself as a person, but particularly about your interaction with others.

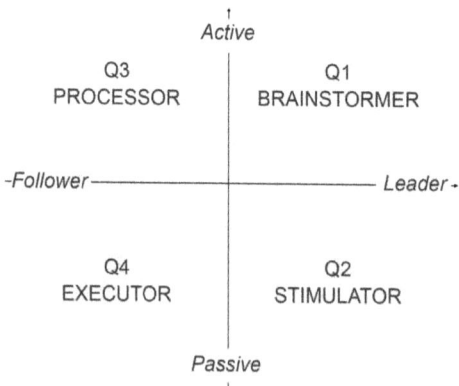

Q1 is a Brainstormer, the active leader who introduces new initiatives. Innovative approaches give them a kick. In groups, they're immediately in the foreground and want to take control. They quickly have a vision, a global approach to tackling problems and will try to win over others for their ideas.

They need to be careful in their enthusiasm that they don't steamroller others and end up standing by themselves and that don't start up one idea after another, without anything happening. The Q1 also doesn't have an eye for detail, which they find uninteresting. They are happy to let others work out the details, just as long as the main idea stays intact.

Q2 is a passive leader and a Stimulator. They guard the whole, feel responsible for that and only act if something isn't going in the right direction. They are ideal support for a Q1. They use the right words at the right moment and encourage the Q1's steps and add to them if needed. They have a sense of responsibility for the whole.

However due to their passive nature, they don't feel like standing on the barricades themselves. They would rather leave that up to others, unless things are really going in the wrong direction, then they will act and take corrective action. Their conscience is their guiding principle for their actions.

Q2s can fall into the trap of becoming too passive. Because of their despondency, they can't find the energy to join in. There's a good chance, however, that they will regret this later.

Q3 is the active developer or Processor. They prefer to work on things from within existing frameworks. Still, they enjoy having something to discuss things with; this makes them feel certain about the right way to proceed. Q3's strength lies in improving an approach from within an existing framework. They optimise existing concepts and have an eye for practical aspects.

The ideal partner for a Q3 is a Q1. However, this can also be a trap. A Q3 dreams of being a Q1, but is unable to be so. This can be the basis for conflicts between them.

Q3 and Q2 together is also not an optimal relationship. The Q2 sees through the lack of leadership in a Q3 and can get annoyed at Q3s attempts to promote themselves as a Q1.

Q3 goes best with a Q4.

Q4 is a Passive Follower or Executor. They are focussed on carrying things out. Initiative is not in their nature, they wait until they are asked. Without any steering from others, they would rather sit and wait. They are really passive by nature and don't want to take any initiative.

If they're asked, then they're happy to help. The best idea is for them to get their instructions from a Q3. These enjoy having a right-hand man to help them carry out their plans. This gives the Q3 a "Q1" feeling.

The Q4 needs management, encouragement and checking, that's when they function best.

A Q1 and Q4 don't get on very well. The Q1 doesn't experience any added value from the Q4 about their own plans, apart from the execution, and they need that.

A Q4 and a Q2 threaten to lapse into passivity, because neither of them wants to take the initiative.

The characteristics of the different Q-types can be described in the following way:

Q1 – Brainstormer: Takes the lead, is dominant and assertive, takes initiative, is prepared to take risks, designs the framework, brings in ideas and concepts, get a kick out of developing new things, is less interested in practical applications and very interested in the whole.

Q2 – Stimulator: Watches over the leader from the side line, using their conscience to do so, doesn't feel the need to be in the spotlight, is long suffering, gives very valuable input, steers when necessary, is the silent powerhouse, watches over the whole, takes the time to do so.

> Q3 – Processor: Powerful implementer and strives for the best solutions within a developed framework, dots the i's and crosses the t's, is a hard worker, can take the lead within a stable domain, seems bossy to others, is a good righthand man and needs discussions with the person with final responsibility.

> Q4 – Executor: Carries out what has been asked and needs clearly defined tasks, functions best through encouragement and checking and needs material advantages.

It's important to know that your Q-Code is your preferred role. That's the role you feel best in, but that isn't to say that you can't take on another role if needs be. That will, however, be less suited to your Soul.

Your Q-Code may be a disappointment. Everyone wants to be Q1 or Q2, but the vast majority of people are Q3 and Q4. Just imagine what a world with only Q1s would be like, it'd be quite a mess. You don't have a Q-Code for nothing. It's a characteristic which suits you in this life and which you need in order to learn from it.

You change Q-Code in each life. That's how your Soul learns how to deal with the different characteristics and you can grow in wisdom.

Each Q-Code has a positive and negative implementation. If you're stressed, under pressure, if you're not feeling at your best, then you'll do the negative side. Take it from me that if you make a mistake in your Age Code and you end up in your Pitfall, then you'll also end up in the negative side of your Q-Code.

So how do you arrive at the correct application of your Q-Code? Well, by getting out of your Pitfall and getting back into reality, by applying your Settler and Stage Phase.

The Q-Code also explains possible tensions in relationships. I've drawn up the above explanation about your Q-Code from the perspective of working in groups.

To let a group function optimally, you need to have the right proportions of all Q-types. This may be an interesting hint for organisations.

But in a relationship, there are only two of you. That is easier in itself but is also more difficult. You can't exactly bring other Q-types in and extend the relationship to a threesome or quadraphonia. That's not how it works.

Proceed from the following point of view, there are no coincidences and what is, is good, otherwise it's different.

Imagine, you request your Relationship-Code with the result that you and your partner are Q2 and Q4. Not an optimal collaboration then, according to what I have indicated above.

But is there's no such thing as a coincidence, so you are in that situation to learn from it. You don't need to conclude from this that you've entered into a bad relationship, even if that is a possibility. You probably have to learn how to deal with the situation. That can lead to one of two conclusions.

Firstly, I'm going to learn to accept myself and the other as they are, so that we can make the best of it.

Second possibility: this is the last straw, it's really not working. It's best to finish this relationship.

That sounds harsh, but let's be clear, I'm not telling you what you should decide. Free will is at play here. What I would like to achieve, is that you are aware of the situation and that you learn to deal with it, learn your life lessons, develop your wisdom. It's your path and you bear your own responsibility for that. You determine what, when, how and with whom, nobody else.

The fundamental conclusion is that you should allow the other to be themselves and not try to change them. Soul Characteristics are a given and are fixed for life.

Know, that if you want to change something in the other, then you need to work on yourself; that makes it possible that the other will change. But that is and always will be the free will of the other person.

This means that the Q-Code in itself doesn't give any judgement about the feasibility of a relationship or when working together, but it does explain some of the difficulties which may arise. Having insights into who you are and who the other is, allows you to deal with these potential traps.

Don't make the mistake of only evaluating your relationship solely based on your Q-Code. Your other characteristics also obviously have a role to play.

Follow your feeling, and ask the question whether your partner really suits you. This takes courage. A lot of people prefer to keep this under wraps. But if there is pressure building up, the pressure will have to be released at some point. Again, this is in your own hands.

So that's why this is a plea for openness. You can only do this by talking, by finding the explanations in the Codes for your attitude and behaviour and by finding the words for how you feel about everything you experience.

That's how mutual understanding and acceptance comes about and these are the foundations for every relationship. In this way, the necessary freedom can emerge and there are no unspoken problems or taboos. This is an important basis for a good relationship.

Freedom within your relationship, makes making love better and more intimate. That's a plus, isn't it? That's another part of unveiling your Soul Path.

Freedom doesn't mean a lack of commitment. In a relationship, you choose each other every day, precisely because of the freedom which you experience. Making this choice is self-evidently, but with freedom comes responsibility.

Z-Code

Your third Relationship-Code is called the Z-Code. This Code indicates the extent to which you can implement your Age Code. This is also a new aspect of the DNA Code, which I'm now explaining for the first time. Why the "Z"? Well, it stands for Soul, in Dutch "Ziel". It tells you whether you are acting often enough in line with you Soul.

What is this characteristic doing in the chapter Relationship-Code? Shouldn't it be in the previous chapter, about the Age Code? Well, that would also be an option, but the key to why you do or don't experience problems implementing your Age Code, is purely a result of your dealings with others. That's why it belongs in the chapter about relationships.

Your Z-Code is namely the result of refusing to implement your Code, out of fear of what others may think. This is a long sentence, which may not sink in straightaway, so read it again if you need to.

Refusing to implement your Age Code has permanent consequences after a while. That may be a shock, but it is what it is and it is good. As you make your bed, so must you lie in it. Once you have accepted that, it's not that bad.

But let me explain how the Z-Code works. You experience a lot of influence from the outside world, even about the extent to which you don't dare to be yourself.

You're afraid that your way of acting won't be accepted or that your way of acting will lead to fractures. These are results, which you would rather ignore. So, you refuse to be who you really are, because of the reactions of others.

That's not how it is supposed to be. You need to learn to be yourself on your path and to accept the consequences of your actions. Know that if you act according to your Soul, the consequences will always be good. By applying your own true self, you are being given a selection of what suits you and what doesn't, after all.

Often acting according to your Soul goes against social norms, upbringing, imprinted pedagogic rules, bad examples etcetera.

The strange thing about fear is that it is based on assumptions. You think that the other won't accept you, you think that acting according to your Soul will have negative consequences. These are all illusions, things that you can't know, because they haven't happened yet.

An example may clarify this. Building further on the earlier example, imagine your Age Code is 2.2, valuing possession and values, but in all your decisions you allow yourself to be led by the outside world.

This means that you aren't determining yourself what is valuable to you. Somewhere there is a fear at play, that if you choose what you find valuable, you won't be appreciated. You're afraid of rejection. You allow your value to depend on others and you refuse to follow your true self out of fear of the consequences of your own choices.

Don't confuse this with a one-time mistake in your Code. Everyone makes mistakes, that's how we learn. No, this is a pertinent refusal because of fear, which means that you don't dare to implement your Code in any way at all.

This is often caused by an intense event, which has shocked you. Because of the fear which ensued, you don't implement your Code at all any more.

Realise that refusal is something you're doing, not something that someone else is doing. You can easily pass on the guilt and feel like a victim, but unfortunately that doesn't work. You and you alone are responsible for your actions. This may be very confrontational, but would you have it any other way?

Back to refusal: if you refuse to implement your Age Code for longer than five years, then this has irreversible consequences. Then your Z-Code is Z3.

During a period of five years of refusal, you are Z2. It's still possible to pick things back up, but as soon as you reach Z3, then you're that way for life. Z1 means that you are doing your Code well, even if you regularly make mistakes.

The characteristics listed in one go:

> **Z1: You are implementing your Age Code in a correct way, even if you make mistakes to learn from.**

> **Z2: You are making mistakes in your Age Code because of refusal and fear of the consequences over a long period of time. An act of will to change your behaviour can bring you to Z1. A long term, incorrect implementation of your Age Code, will result in you becoming Z3.**

> **Z3: You have refused to carry out your Age Code over a long period of time and you haven't implemented it because of fear of the consequences. The result of this is that you have difficulties with achieving your Code and finding the meaning of life. You can still find a reason for your existence in spirituality. To achieve your Soul Growth, you will have to keep trying to carry out your Age Code well. Support can help you do this. The Z3 characteristic is permanent.**

> **Z4: You have not sought any insights from setbacks over a long period of time, your Soul Growth will remain slow.**

> **Z5: Your constant resistance to your Age Code through negative behaviour leads to you not seeking any more insights.**

This overview might be a little shocking. So be aware: Z4 and Z5 are the unconscious ones. It would amaze me if they were to read this book to gain insights. But first let me go into Z2 and Z3 a little.

Be aware that the vast majority of society are Z3s, about 4 out of 5 people you come across. That's a bit of a shock, isn't it? Naturally your automatic reaction is: what about me then? Well, don't draw any hasty conclusions, but be realistic. If you want to know the answer, request your Code.

Your Z-Code determines how you live your life. Refusal to apply your Code isn't without consequences. The Z2 experiences a feeling of lack of direction and unease. The basis for this behaviour is fears. These prevent them from applying their Code. Fears are in the head, they are delusions. The Z2 doesn't see the advantages of applying their Code, only the possible negative consequences. These don't fit with reality. It is important that the Z2 learns to see through their fears.

You do this by accepting your fears, by allowing doom scenarios and then seeing through them and realising that these are delusions.

The only way to do this is to concentrate on concrete experiences and to ask yourself why you are refusing to apply your Code. Why are you scared? Which consequences prevent you from applying your Code?

After a period of five years as a Z2, becoming Z3 first leads to peacefulness and resignation. Still the Z3 characteristic has direct consequences. It becomes more difficult to make concrete steps in accordance with your Code. Refusal is now permanent. If you have support and focus on a small step, you may be able to take some steps.

Through not being successful in applying their Code, Z3s experience a form of despondency. They can't see any meaning to life anymore, because they don't experience the satisfaction which comes from implementing their Age Code correctly. They do experience great satisfaction in spirituality and that grows into their life aim, it gives their life meaning.

The consequence for Z3s and Z2s is that they spend a lot of time in their Pitfall. In fact, an incorrect application of your Age Code always leads to this result. This does have a positive side as well. Z2s and Z3s learn to deal with their PitfallS better, which is also a part of your Soul Mission. Every cloud has a silver lining. It's just a matter of how you look at it.

The greatest disadvantage for the Z3 is that they feel like a victim of what happens in their lives. This is linked to their despondency, which leads them to ascribing the causes of everything as being outside themselves.

But as always, you are both cause and effect. Your Z3-ness is a result of your own actions.

For both Z2 as well as Z3, it is a good idea that they receive support to learn how to deal with this characteristic. In this way, Z3s can learn to deal with their feelings of being a victim and how to implement things in the material world. And Z2s learn to deal with their fears and how to become Z1 again if possible.

Often the moment at which the refusal takes place, provides insights into the reason why. The cause might be a traumatic experience.

Be careful about investigating how this came about by yourself. You may have a suspicion about why you didn't apply the Code as a child, for example. But everyone makes mistakes in their Code. Don't confuse this with a pertinent refusal. This means that you refuse to apply your Code in any domain.

The Z-Code can appear in each Age Code. If you become Z2, then you can become Z1 by breaking through this refusal. This seems simple, but in practise it's often difficult; it's an inner process, an emotional change in yourself.

A few practical explanations:

- If you change your Age Code as a Z2 (at 12, 18 or 36) then you start the next part of your DNA Code as a Z1. This has no further consequences. You may have acquired less experience in developing your talent, but you can catch up with that later.

- If you are a Z2 and you successfully recover and then become a Z1, then this is a permanent characteristic. You can't go backwards. It's like learning to cycle or swim, once you've learned it, you can't unlearn it.
- Whether you are a Z1, Z2 or Z3, your Soul Growth doesn't need to suffer because of it. Growing in wisdom is open to everyone, if you keep trying to apply your Age Code. That is difficult for Z2 and Z3. However, if they try and keep looking for insights, then they can grow in wisdom without any problems. How you grow in wisdom will be explained in the chapter Evolution Mission.
- Z2 and Z3 refuse to apply their Code in every facet of their lives. A Z1 succeeds at applying their true self correctly in at least 1 area.

So, now you know enough about Z2s and Z3s. Then there are also Z4s and Z5s. They aren't searching for insights, they've already given up.

Specific to a Z5 is that they give up during puberty. They've only applied the negative side of their Pitfall and that results in a negative attitude to everything.

Z4 are like headless chickens, sorry for the expression, but it's a fact. They experience life as pointless and live from day to day, unconsciously, without any kind of contentment.

They find life a drag and don't ask any questions about it. It's a form of vegetation, the grey masses.

Your Z-Code gives you important insights into yourself. You're not aware of your Z-Code. Everyone often spends time in their Pitfall due to mistakes against their Age Code. So, it's difficult to work out for yourself whether this is permanent.

That's why it is useful to ask for your Z-Code and if desired, to receive guidance to learn how to deal with this characteristic. This will definitely prove very fruitful.

C-Code & Sphere Fear

In addition to the fear for the consequences of implementing your Code, your Z-Code, there are other fears which can cause you difficulties. These are represented by your C-Code and your Sphere Fear. These are your fundamental fears which prevent you from implementing your Age Code correctly in specific circumstances.

Again, this Code has to do with relationships. You develop these fears very specifically when dealing with others.

Again, it is a totally new aspect of the DNA Code, which I am explaining here for the first time.

You may know your astrological fears, represented by Pallas in your natal horoscope. These are fears which are true individually. Your C-Code is different to this and works in relation to others. I hope that prevents any possible confusion.

I want to pay more attention to dealing with fears later and only discuss the main aspects here. It is extremely important to be able to confront your fears, allow them in, accept them and then deal with them.

Your C-Code fears are inherited from your previous lives. See them as primeval fears: the fear of not being enough, the fear of not being seen, the fear of change, the fear of having to cope with things alone. These are some examples of primeval fears which can cause you difficulties.

Fear paralyses you and drives your thinking. That's how ideas, delusions, which have nothing to do with the real world come into being. It's a result of your over-active fantasy. It prevents you from being who you really are.

Because of your fears, you're no longer inhabiting the real world. Your feet aren't on the ground, because that is exactly what you are afraid of. This leads to a virtual reality. You live inside your fears, which are very real to you, even if your experience doesn't fit the real world.

The C-Code consists of 12 fear groups. The reason I'm calling these groups, is because fears can have various facets which can be bundled into one heading. For example, you're afraid of loneliness, but a variation on this is the fear of being superfluous or the fear of losing your children. These are variations on the same theme.

Of the 12 fears, 2 of them create difficulties for you. They distract you from your authentic self, which means that you're implementing your DNA Code incorrectly. Through this, the waterfall of incorrect implementation of your whole Birth Code is initiated.

Overview of the C-Codes:
- **1: The fear of bodily harm.**
- **2: The fear of not having enough.**
- **3: The fear of being misunderstood.**
- **4: The fear of not belonging.**
- **5: The fear of not being seen.**
- **6: The fear of becoming unemployed.**
- **7: The fear of being on your own.**
- **8: The fear of being excluded.**
- **9: The fear of believing in the wrong things.**
- **10: The fear of having no place in society.**
- **11: The fear of being restricted in your freedom.**
- **12: The fear of being forced.**

It's a long list and you might have been touched by it just through reading. That's good news, because it is the start of your becoming conscious. You can't change anything that you're not conscious of. If you're conscious of your fear, then you can learn to deal with it.

If you remain in the realm of the unconscious, then you won't realise how this is causing you difficulties and you'll be led by your fear, without even knowing it. Again, it's a conscious choice to choose a conscious life and that requires an act of will. That's how you unveil your Soul Path.

Your primeval fears can be turned into strengths, by experiencing your fears and deflating them. Doom scenarios help with this; blow them up into something enormous and then burst them.

After you've imagined the worst possible situation, you'll see that this has no link with reality. This puts your feet firmly back on the ground and you'll find out that your fears were really an illusion.

That's how you learn to turn your fears around and to no longer experience any problems with them. It helps you to see your Soul Path, your fear is like mist which obscures your path. Don't let yourself be distracted and learn how to deal with this.

Sphere Fear:

In addition to the C-Code there are also Sphere Fears. You also experience a specific fear, according to your Sphere Behaviour, your Birth Sphere.

The First Sphere has a fundamental fear of not surviving, a real fear of death. This can lead to panicky reactions, over the top reactions, the struggle for life. This explains their dependence. When all's said and done, focusing on another is a survival strategy. By becoming aware of this, you can temper your dependence.

A Second Sphere has the fear of losing control if they behave according to their feelings. They are afraid that this will disadvantage them, because they won't be able to steer from their rational mind any more. They need to learn that acting from their feelings will bring them more advantages than disadvantages.

The Third Sphere is afraid of humiliation. They want to raise themselves and others up to a higher level, but are afraid that they will run into trouble and be humiliated if they are not successful. This can prevent them from trying to elevate themselves and others.

First Sphere-fear: Fear of death

Second Sphere-fear: Fear of losing control

Third Sphere-fear: Fear of humiliation

Once again, each of these fears is an illusion, they keep you away from your true self. They transport you to a virtual reality, the world of fears. They seem real and you experience them as real, but they aren't.

I'll discuss fears again further on this book in the chapter about Cleansing. First, I would like to complete the Soul Missions and talk about your Evolution Mission and your Personal Mission.

EVOLUTION MISSION

Now that you know all about your Birth Code, Age Code and other Soul Characteristics, it's time for the next important part of your Soul Mission, namely your Soul Evolution. There are quite some misunderstandings about this and some new aspects to be told.

Your Evolution Code is a very specific way of gaining in wisdom. You could say that it is an extension of your Birth Code. That's because you experience an inner desire to keep learning. You do that in many ways, the basis is your life experiences, your coincidences and your insights, ...

All these experiences allow you to grow. They help you discover your true self and to become more and more yourself.

This is expressed in, **amongst other things**, your Evolution Code. "Amongst other things" is in bold for a good reason. I've done this to stress the relative nature and the importance of the Evolution Code.

Evolution Code is important, but it isn't the whole story. It shows how you grow further in wisdom and how you can actually apply this wisdom. This Code doesn't however tell you if you will really do so. Knowing how to do something right is completely different than doing the right thing.

Growing in wisdom is a little like learning a life lesson. You do so because of an experience you've had. The key word here is living through it and you do that by feeling, thinking and doing. All three elements are necessary to fully internalise an experience.

You may recognise the Types which were explained earlier and you would be right. You start your experience in your own Type, but there are two conditions to internalise an experience.

Firstly, you need to finish with a feeling, which gives you an sentimental conclusion. Secondly, you need to have gone around the Type Circle at least once. This means that you need to take various steps before you really get something.

For example, a Thinker thinks, does and feels, and then thinks about their feelings to determine what the best thing to do is. Doing gives them a "feeling of closure". Here they experience the results of their actions and they receive a confirmation that they have or haven't done the right thing.

This all seems a little complicated, but you do all of this on an unconscious level. You learn intuitively that the trick works like this. Rome wasn't built in a day: you'll learn to apply this quicker and better once you've understood it.

It's good to know that you need to experience something several times before you'll have really understood it. On average, you'll need to learn a lesson three times before you really understand it through and through.

The result is that you have then added a piece of wisdom to your conscience. You've learned to apply it in a correct way and you're able, in principle, to apply the right way of acting according to your Soul from now on.

But there's a fly in the ointment here:

It's good not to forget what is known.

You people are very good at forgetting things when it suits you. I call that stupidity: knowing what to do and still not doing it.

That's why the wisdom levels in your Evolution Code tell you nothing about the extent to which you're applying your lessons. It only indicates the level of the wisdom you've accrued.

You sometimes come across someone who seems to feel good in their own skin, serene, themselves, no games, ... You might conclude that this person is very wise. That might well be true, but it might possibly be someone who is able to apply their own wisdom, and that's something completely different.

So, don't let yourself get trapped by the Evolution Code. It tells you something about your accrued wisdom, but if you don't act accordingly, it is a meaningless measurement!

Now that you know this, I'd like to tell you something about the difference between Seekers and Finders. That's because the Evolution Mission is different for Seekers and Finders.

The Finder has chosen to focus solely on their Birth Mission in this life and to do this in a straightforward way. They don't have an Evolution Code, like a Seeker does.

However, a Finder can achieve Soul Growth. They do this by mastering their Birth Code in all possible facets. There's a growth scheme for this, which is different than for Seekers. I'm not going to explain this further. That's because the number of Finders who would like to go into this at depth is limited to a few individuals.

We do live in special times, so the number of Finders who choose "consciousness" may increase over the coming years. You never know. When the time is ripe, I'll provide the information required.

Know now that a Finder who chooses growth can evolve into a Seeker. It's the only characteristic in your Birth Code which can change during your lifetime. They'll need to learn all aspects of their Code to do so.

As soon as they become a Seeker, they'll initially need to make a massive adjustment. Someone who becomes a Seeker as an adult, is confronted by what a Seeker learned intuitively as a child.

It's a very exciting experience, but only for those who have the courage to take this path. The choice also leads to great satisfaction.

Then the Seeker, the name speaks for itself. The big difference between Seekers and Finders is that the Seeker was born with the Soul Mission of growing in wisdom. They are always "seeking" and looking for as many variations as possible.

This is expressed in the Evolution Code, which is an addition to your Age Code. This is a very important basis. You can only grow by focussing on your Age Code.

Your Evolution Code shows you variations in which you apply your Age Code. See it as a series of angles which gives additional insights into your Code.

Your Birth Code is the final point which you reached in your evolution in your previous life and your starting point for this life. So, as a Seeker, you get the chance to tackle another piece of your Soul Path.

Your Evolution Code is an important part of your Soul Path. It tells you how far you've already come on your path. Life after life, you grow in wisdom through the Spheres.

If your Birth Sphere Step is 2.2 then you'll then go on to apply 2.3. If you've experienced this enough, 2.4 will follow.

The Evolution Code is described in detail by your Sphere Step of Evolution and the Stage Phase of Evolution. This Code also consists of the previously stated 21 steps.

So, if you were born as a 2.2, then you'll focus on everything to do with possession and valuation. If you evolve onto 2.3, then you'll learn how to do 2.2 according to your feelings. The following step, 2.4, is then learning to set boundaries to possession and valuation. In this way, you'll carry on refining your Birth Mission.

You go through all the Stage Phases in every Sphere Step of Evolution in a specific order. See this as the 21 variations on the Sphere Step of Evolution. It's a second level of refinement which teaches you to further improve your Age Code.

How you do this is represented step by step in the growth scheme at the back of this book. You may get confused by the numbers, so the following should make this clear.

Stage Phase of Evolution 1.3 is a higher number than 3.1. That's because each last number increases from 1 to 7 and you do three steps in each. For the first step, this means that you do 1.1, 2.1 and 3.1 consecutively, to progress onto 1.2, 2.2 and 3.2.

This might seem complicated so I'll repeat it one more time: don't focus too hard on your Evolution Code, because if you forget to apply your Birth Code, you won't learn anything.

Your Soul Growth isn't a competition either. One person grows faster than another. Everyone does this at their own speed. So, don't apply a value judgement to it. Don't let yourself get caught up in comparisons with others, that's always an incorrect attitude by the way.

I'd like to give you one more important addition to the growth scheme. Just as in the introduction, I've limited myself to the first 3 Spheres. But it doesn't stop there.

There are more, namely 7 Spheres. These Spheres are part of Cosmic Degrees. There are 7 of these as well.

So, now you're getting a first peek at the greater whole, 7 Cosmic Degrees, each built up out of 7 Spheres. That's the path which every Soul takes. You might find this very exciting, as it indeed is.

I've already indicated that you go through the first three Spheres in the material world, here on earth. These are part of the 3rd Cosmic Degree. As soon as you've evolved into the Fourth Sphere, you won't incarnate any more.

The number of growers is increasing noticeably. Some tens of people on earth have already gone beyond the Third Sphere. That's why it's important for these people as well to make a manual for how they can best struggle through these higher Spheres in the material world. But this is the basis for another book.

I'd like to say that even for those that haven't arrived in the higher Spheres yet, that this is very useful information. That's because you can already learn lessons from this which will be very useful to you in your everyday life.

This brings us to the subject of "fast" growth. The question is often posed, how can you grow in wisdom as quickly as possible? I would like to repeat that the Evolution Code isn't a competition. If you want to prove yourself through this, then you are going about things in completely the wrong way.

There are some tips for growing in wisdom. Put your feelings into words, look for insights, apply your life lessons in practise, accept reality, don't let yourself get distracted by your fears and learn to deal with your Ego and your rational mind.

Growing in wisdom is a confrontation with yourself. This requires courage and persistence. The key terms are feelings, putting into words, insights, acceptance and acts of will. It's not just about knowing, but about applying.

The definition of stupidity is not applying what you actually know. A correct insight only arrives when you feel it. So, no growth without feeling.

What happens if your Evolution Code goes into the next Sphere? Then you'll also learn the characteristics of that Sphere. From the third step of the next Sphere, you'll have internalised the corresponding Sphere Behaviour. If you were born a First Sphere, you can differeniate from 2.3 onwards. As a Second Sphere, you have really understood elevating from 3.3 onwards. You then learn how to do your Age Code from this new Sphere Behaviour.

If you make a mistake in your Birth Code, then you'll fall back into your Birth Sphere Behaviour. Your birth characteristics are and will remain your foundation.

If you evolve to the Third Sphere, your Birth Pitfall changes as well. Throughout the First and Second Sphere, you've had the time to practise your Birth Pitfall enough, but you've also accumulated new mistakes. They're summarised in a new Pitfall-Code to practise in. Here again, you regress to your Birth Pitfall during times of stress.

Until now, I've stressed the aspect of insight in order to grow in wisdom. That's the optimal way to grow. You can however also grow in another way, unconsciously or as a dreamer.

You can simply grow by experiencing setbacks. This automatically leads to emotional experiences. On an unconscious level, this leads to a slow growth. Without realising it, you are learning from the experiences which you have been through. The vast majority of people grow in this way. They are the unconscious ones, who still evolve a few small steps in each life.

A second group of growers does this through imagination. They don't have their feet firmly on the ground, but learn lessons through their thoughts. That's possible, but then you're a dreamer. It allows your wisdom to grow slowly, because you don't have any personal experiences in reality.

Insights from concrete experiences are required if you want to communicate your insights to others - call it Mastery. This is the ideal way to grow in wisdom. Without your own experiences, you can't guide others. Then you're basing yourself on your fantasy and that's not the correct point of reference.

Keeping your feet on the ground and consciously looking for insights is a requirement to grow in wisdom.

Then I'd like to do away with some misunderstandings. Growing in wisdom is too often confused with being Ego-less and Karma-less. That's not correct. By growing in wisdom, you learn how to better deal with your Ego and Karma, but you don't solve anything.

This distinction is very important. That's why I've set out the various parts of the unveiling of your Soul Path in this book. Ultimately, they're one whole. On the other hand, you then threaten to lump everything together, so that's why it's important to keep things separate. If you've understood the parts, then you'll discover their connections.

Eastern wisdom hammers on about letting go of the Ego. Their solution is to withdraw from society. But what if we were all to do that? I hope that you notice the cynicism in my question. Quite obviously, society would disappear if we were all to withdraw from it. Only then, there would be a new one with the same problems.

So that's not a good solution. It's better to learn to deal with your Ego in society. It's a part of you. I'll explain how you learn to deal with it in the next chapter.

The same is true of your Karma. Growing in wisdom is one thing, but cleansing your Karma is something completely different. See it as two different trails on your Soul Path. The only connection is that applying the wisdom you've gained teaches you how to cleanse it better.

The conclusion of this chapter Evolution Code, is that it's a very important part of your Soul Path. But it doesn't tell you anything about your applied wisdom. It's the only Code which shows your progress in gaining wisdom.

After this comes the essence of spirituality, learning how to apply this in all areas of your life. These experiences will give you additional insights and refinements.

Is there an end to this growth, does it ever stop? Well, I have to burst this illusion as well. Often people think that 3.7 is the end point and from there on in, you've reached Heaven on Earth.

3.7 is also called enlightenment. This is a dangerous term, however, which may cause you to dream of a continual feeling of ecstasy.

Take the term enlightenment literally. In 3.7 you feel lighter, if you know how to apply your wisdom, but there is no change in the lightness of being.

So, I'll have to bring you back down to earth again. Heaven on Earth consists of a combination of pleasant and unpleasant experiences, of making mistakes and gaining new insights as a result. You can always learn more. There is no end point to wisdom.

This wouldn't match with the philosophy of the Soul. Do you remember? In the first chapter, I explained the little speck of God within you. You experience your inner strength in order to keep searching for insights. This is your contribution to the Greater Oneness, something that you feel a part of.

In this way, you discover deeper layers within yourself, refine experiences and feelings and, step by step, discover how you can stay closer to who you really are.

You learn how this trick works again and again. The wisdom you are gaining is a way of acting, how you can tackle things. There are endless new lessons to be learned. This may seem discouraging, but you are never finished! So, how do you know what you need to learn?

To do this, make use of coincidences which occur, then you'll know what to do. Each experience can bring you additional insights. This is linked to the endless possible growth in wisdom.

So, wisdom is knowing how! If you've completed a Sphere Step, then you are actually standing at the very start of applying it.

For example, you were born a 2.2 and you've completed the evolution Sphere Step 2.4. So, you're starting on 2.5. What do you know about 2.4? Well, you've learned how to apply 2.4 correctly, but that doesn't mean that you're completely finished with 2.4. From now on, you'll need to apply it all the time and to refine it for yourself further. You do this while you're working on the next step: 2.5.

You could say that 2.4 is extra help for doing 2.5. That's applying your wisdom.

Know as well that by applying your wisdom your path becomes narrower. Since you know how to do so, there's less room to manoeuvre. This means that you make mistakes more quickly and in this way, you learn more.

I'd like to tell you something about unconditional surrender, the famous 3.7. Think about these words for a moment. What do they mean exactly? Literally, they mean that you place no conditions on your surrender, you learn to only act in accordance with your Soul.

Does that mean that you'll always do this, every time and everywhere? No, just that you've learned in 3.7 how to deal with it. You'll encounter every theme and subject which you need to apply this to, after 3.7. This lesson is true of every Sphere Step.

3.7 is actually the Abstinence Sphere, as you're learning how to release your urges, because urges are conditional. When you have an urge, you are also building in a condition at the same time. That's an exercise in power. You want to achieve your urge, which is the opposite of surrender.

What exactly is surrender? It's acceptance of what is. That's the basis. You don't resist what's happening to you. Don't confuse this with fatalism, it doesn't mean that you need to undergo all kinds of things.

Surrender means that you allow the moment to be the most it can be for you. It entails taking your fate in your own hands, taking acts of will, not being someone's puppet, but taking the wheel yourself.

That's also a process in growing in wisdom, sticking up for yourself in line with your Soul. It requires courage, a strong will and persistence. I don't want to put you off, even if that may be the consequence of me saying this.

Know that once you start on your Soul Path that it's like planting a seed. It's a very hardy seed, with unstoppable strength which can only carry you forwards. You'll experience not wanting to go backwards, because you know it's good. In this way, you can experience your Soul Wish to keep growing, looking for insights, refining your feelings and applying your wisdom.

I don't need to encourage you to do that. Your inner God will take care of that, for you have a Soul which inevitably wants to experience its development. The next step will teach you a lot about this. Now it's becoming completely personal!

PERSONAL SOUL MISSION

Are you ready for the next piece of the pie? I'd like to talk about your Personal Soul Mission, another new aspect. As stated earlier, I want to put the entire story to paper. So, buckle in for the next part of your Soul Missions.

You have a Personal Soul Mission along with your Birth Mission and Evolution Mission. Your Soul has a set of specific tasks to carry out in this life.

These can be very diverse, for example: learning how to enjoy yourself, learning how to deal with loneliness, learning to stick up for yourself, learning how to confront yourself in all kinds of ways, learning how to deal with responsibilities, learning how to be yourself in a group, to name but a few.

Your Personal Soul Mission gives you a list of specific things which you want to tackle in this life. I can hear you thinking, 'Oops, what might my mission be?' Don't worry, you know more than you realise.

How can you find out what that mission is? The answer is quite simplistic and complex at the same time. You'll find out by following your Soul, by engaging with the coincidences you encounter, by differentiating between what you really want and what you don't. Then you'll automatically be applying this mission.

I'd like to underline that you don't need to know your Personal Soul Mission. So, don't start wondering what yours might be. By accepting who you are and the circumstances in which you live, you are automatically working on your mission.

We in the Spirit World will present you with the coincidences you need so that you can implement your Soul Mission; you have the choice whether to engage with them.

If you'd like something concrete, focus on something which you have the most difficulty with, something you really dislike. There's a good chance that this reflects your Personal Mission.

You may be wondering whether you choose your Personal Mission yourself or whether it is imposed? Well, that's difficult to grasp from the material world, but if your Soul resided in the Spirit World, you'd experience the wish of the Greater Oneness as your own wish.

There is no difference between what you want as a Soul and what the Greater Oneness wants. There is no negotiation or anything like that, about your next mission. It's a logical conclusion.

You may start your life mission with some reluctance. You may experience that in regressions, but you still know that it's good for you and your Soul agrees with your mission.

Your previous lives determine your Personal Soul Mission. If you expressed too much power in a previous life, than you may choose to experience the other side in this life. This brings you to a place where you have to submit to power a lot.

Your place of birth is a first choice in this. You choose the circumstances which allow you to gain the right wisdom at a later age. This is a good indication of what you have to learn.

Know that you often end up in an opposite situation. As a child, you might mainly see how it shouldn't be done and experience what you need to learn so that you can do it differently yourself.

But keep your feet on the ground, don't start floating off, live in the reality of the here and now. Even if your past has coloured you, you can't change anything about it. Your memory goes no further than this life, you can only draw lessons from this one.

Let's return to your Personal Soul Mission. Another way to approach this in a simple way, is to make a distinction between authentic and inauthentic. You recognise authentic people immediately. That's how you want to be yourself. So, go and look for your authentic self.

Actually, you know very well when you're playing games, have the wrong intentions, are acting from expectations. An uneasy feeling in your body is an indication of disbalance. It's a sign of inauthenticity.

Often people say that they have a special mission, an exalted aim and that's often ridiculous. Many have the feeling that they need to save the world and feel chosen to do so.

Know that everyone is chosen and that you do indeed have a special mission. Your Soul Mission is to discover your own authentic self and to apply it, to live in accordance with your Soul and to grow in wisdom.

Focusing on others without looking at yourself in the mirror is completely wrong. Let's be clear, saving Souls is definitely not your mission. You can't save another Soul; every Soul has to do that for themselves.

You can only offer insights if a question comes. If it doesn't, then don't preach! Because, before you know it, you'll be exercising power. Many feel called to express a message, which I or another gave to them, but look before you leap.

It's part of your Soul Mission to do this by being an example for others, by taking your Soul Path yourself. That's how you express the Message and how you can inspire others, but that's not the aim. You are doing this for yourself!

What do I mean by the Message? Actually, that's the complete content of this book. You're expressing the Message by living in accordance with your Soul, no more and no less.

So, there are no openings for preachers and vicars in this book, nor for bishops or cardinals, not even for a Pope. These only lead to power structures.

Often the idea of being chosen is driven from the Ego: the need to prove yourself, to have prestige. This brings us to an important subject in the Soul Path, love versus power.

Your Soul is disgusted by exercising or submitting to power. Part of your Soul Path is gaining power over yourself, not wanting to exercise power over others and not undergoing influence from others.

This is an extremely difficult part of your Soul Path and, in the first instance, seems virtually impossible, However, it is a clear Soul Wish.

Without having exercised or having to submit to power, you don't know how it works. You can't let something go without having experienced it. We call this the Ego-cycle, which you go through in every life.

After you have used your Ego a lot as an adolescent, your Soul wants to take over your Ego at a certain point in time. Many feel this inner desire but don't know how to apply it. Another phrase for this is a midlife crisis.

Ego means wanting to meet others' expectations, including those of society. Your Soul wants you to act according to your own norms and values and this leads to a serious confrontation; you may come up against things which are not socially acceptable at all. Then the most difficult thing of all occurs, namely the act of will to follow your Soul and to accept the consequences of your actions.

This is where a lot of people trip up. You go to family parties because it's expected, while you really don't want to, do you? Why do you do that? Discovering your Soul Path means that you drop what you don't yourself want.

Real love is choosing freedom and allowing the other to have the freedom to make their own choices. If these don't agree with your own opinions, then you have to accept that. That's how you learn what suits you and what doesn't.

If you want to express the Message to others, be an example by being yourself. Don't try to change your environment or save it, don't comment on what others are doing, but begin with yourself.

But what if following your true self seems to harm others? Let's return to the examples of the parties where you don't feel good. Imagine that you don't go any more, then it will hurt your family, won't it? There is indeed a good chance of that, but know if you follow your true self you can never damage others.

The impact of your actions on another is no more and no less than what the other needs in order to learn from it themselves.

If your family forces you to go, then they're exercising power over you and they're not allowing you to be free to make your own choices. If you don't go, they're confronted by their own actions and they get a chance to learn from this themselves.

This is true of every form of confrontation. Expressing your anger, not to hurt someone, but simply because you feel anger, is pure love. It means that you think the other is worth your while to share your own feelings with. That can only create clarity. For the other, it's a chance to gain their own insights.

The key is the intention of your choice, namely why you're doing something. If you aren't going to parties in revenge for frustration about an event, then you're going about things in completely the wrong way.

But how do you know what you really want? You'll learn that by a process of trial and error, by following your feelings, by looking at coincidences and by applying the sum of everything in this book.

It's not an easy thing because of the ballast which you are carrying around, but for the Soul it's very simple. You really want to or you really don't want to. There isn't any compromise. Let's be clear about that.

The basis for this is expressing your feelings and searching for your insights. Clearing ballast can help you with this. That's what the next chapter is about.

CLEANSING BALLAST

As I've already said: you carry a lot of ballast around with you which keeps you from your authentic self and from finding your Soul Path. Part of unveiling your path is dealing with and reducing obstacles such as Karma, fear, your rational mind and Ego.

That's why in this chapter I'm going to go further into each of these subjects and I'll teach you to cleanse them. Dealing with intentions, norms and values, intentions and expectations is of essential importance in this area.

Know that acting against your Soul cannot remain without any consequences. Not only for your Soul but also for your body. In particular, if you persist in refusing to act while you know better, you'll experience setbacks. The aim of this is to still spur you into action. I'll come back to this later.

I'd like to discuss intolerance as an introduction to this chapter. How tolerant are you? What irritates you in other people? Think about this. You'll come to the conclusion that you have a number of intolerances, things which you are sensitive to, which irritate you, which you find difficult to bear.

Hold on tight, because your intolerance towards others shows you something about yourself. It tells you what you need to work on yourself! Sobering thought? Let me give you an example.

Imagine that you find it really difficult to deal with inflexible people, that they really irritate you. That means that you need to work on your own inflexibility. Another example, if you find it difficult when people play the victim, then that's probably a pattern which you often apply yourself.

So, the other tells you something about yourself. That's a revelation. It brings you back to the essence, to yourself. It makes you stand in front of the mirror and reflect on how that all works in yourself. At least, it does if you want to live consciously.

Let me give you a tip about dealing with your own intolerances. Learn to accept the other's attitude. Accept, for example, that the other can be inflexible. If you can take this step, you might be able to accept your own inflexibility.

For whatever you can't see or recognise in yourself, stays in your unconscious. You can't change the unconscious.

As stated earlier, unveiling your Soul Path is actually a process of becoming conscious. As soon as you're conscious of something in yourself, you can get to work on it. Whatever is unconscious, stays unconscious and unchanged.

Several elements can play a role in intolerance: your fears, your Ego, your rational mind, patterns which you have unconsciously taken over from bad role models, your own idiosyncratic way of protecting yourself from your environment, your unprocessed feelings from the past. There's a long list of possibilities, which I'll be explaining further in the coming chapters.

So, let's go with the flow and tackle the first source of annoyance, your Karma.

Cleansing Karma

I've already explained what Karma is. See it as the sum of experiences from which you haven't learned your lessons and about which you haven't expressed your feelings. It's ballast which keeps you from your true self. This will become clear later.

Building up and reducing Karma is part of your Soul Path. It's way of living. Everyone makes mistakes and builds Karma up, in order to learn how to reduce it as part of their growth in wisdom. You could easily call cleansing Karma a Soul Mission.

You can see your ballast as a burden, a punishment from God, but also as an opportunity. Each day you receive several chances to reduce your ballast. You come across coincidences which give you an emotional experience. If the experience is one of fulfilment, then you know that is a good. If it's an unpleasant feeling, then you get the chance to clear something away.

There are no bad feelings, because you also need unpleasant feelings. If you combine these with cleansing, then this will lead to a pleasant experience. So, an unpleasant experience can lead to fulfilment!

Let me tell you how your feeling comes into being. Your Soul reflects whether something is good or bad in every situation. An experience is in line with your Soul or not in line with your Soul. This good/bad experience is the basis for your feelings. This gives you pleasant or unpleasant feelings, such as: connectedness, fulfilment, ecstasy, loneliness, anger, sadness, ...

Don't confuse feeling with emotions. A feeling is translated into an emotion if you refuse to feel. Often crying, yelling and non-verbal behaviour are expressions which are the result of not feeling. But if you really feel, then you won't slip into emotions.

Emotions are often a way of wielding power, of attracting

attention, of influencing your environment. That's why it's better to be alone when you let your emotions run free. Then you can be certain that you are not wielding power over another.

Now back to cleansing, you do this in 5 steps. This rule of 5 is the key to experiencing spirituality consciously and to keeping your feet firmly on the ground. You can apply it to any situation, at any time. It helps you grow in wisdom, to gain clarity over your Soul Path, to discover your authenticity, but above all to learn how to apply your wisdom.

I can't underline the importance of this facet enough; real spirituality is applying your Soul Path in practise. Knowing, without applying, is pure stupidity.

CLEANSING STEP 1: FEELING

The first step is feeling fully. You do this in a concrete situation and preferably at that very moment. Feel what something does to you, breathe towards your stomach, be aware of what you are experiencing. This is an all-encompassing attitude to life, this is where consciousness begins.

You can practise this. If aren't yet able to do this, you can take time at the end of each day to ask yourself what happened and what feelings did I experience with each event. What did I enjoy? What didn't I enjoy? When did I feel ok? When didn't I feel ok?

You can try to recall the experience by putting yourself back into the situation as it were, by recalling what happened. You might then discover which feelings you missed.

This exercise teaches you to shorten the time between the realisation of the feeling and the event itself, until you can be aware of the effect that something has on you at that exact moment.

If you can't do that yet, start talking during the event. Use the words "what effect is this having on me, what am I feeling...", even if you don't yet know what you are feeling. It will become clear to you through talking, look for the words and you will find them. That's how you learn to feel, it requires an act of will.

I've already explained the Circle of Types. So, you know that you have to go around at least once before you can arrive at a final feeling. See talking as a form of doing, which brings you closer to your feeling. It's a bridge to the next step in cleansing.

CLEANSING STEP 2: EXPRESSING

The second step is expressing your feelings. This is necessary. You can express them out loud to yourself, possibly to your partner or a friend. The ideal is to express your feelings then and there. Expression gives you clarity. Try to explain how you experience your feelings as broadly as possible. While talking, which is a form of doing, additional facets of your experience will emerge. Without talking, these won't rise to the surface.

Expressing your feeling also releases the tension from the experience. If you express yourself, do it with feeling, not from your rational mind. Experiencing your feelings when expressing them is crucial, that way you can live and feel through the experience.

An additional advantage of expressing your feelings in the moment, or possibly later, is creating clarity for your environment. Express your feeling without any hidden agenda, without wanting to hurt the other, without wanting to teach them a lesson, without wanting to achieve anything by doing so.

The only correct attitude is to say what something does to you, without blaming the other.

Let me give you an example. Your child is naughty and that makes you angry. Expressing your anger to your child can easily get dangerous. If you say, "because of you I'm angry" then you are mistreating your child.

This is misusing your feelings to manipulate and correct your child. Your child might conclude, Mum is angry so I'm bad and might mistakenly internalise the idea that you have to correct people through anger.

If a child oversteps a rule, then you have the right to be angry. Say how you feel if rules are broken. That makes it clear to the child that the anger is linked to the misstep.

Dealing with expressing feelings is always good if you are talking about your own feelings. You can't have a rational argument about this, your feelings are your feelings.

The following statement explains this:

Expressing feelings is fine, if you don't do it to undermine!

So, say what you are feeling without blaming the other. This takes some practise. You can make the link to the other's behaviour and then explain which feelings this provokes in you. Nothing more, nothing less.

Take a while to think about the sense and desirability of expressing your feelings to another. If it doesn't make any sense or isn't desirable, then don't express them to that person, but to yourself or a third party.

Imagine your mother is in her early nineties and is dying. You still feel frustration about your upbringing as a child. Are you going to rub her nose in it again? This example is extreme, but it shows how this trick works. Ask yourself the question: will expressing my feelings to the person involved really make sense and is it desirable? This will make you aware of your intentions for expressing them.

So, expressing your feeling is not a blind dogma, but an essential part of who you are, which you should approach in a conscious manner.

Don't underestimate the impact of expressing or not expressing your feelings. Imagine, you experience a situation which makes you very angry, but you don't express it. Your anger will remain in your body.

This will trigger you into different behaviour. You'll express your "angriness" in other ways. You'll become surly, intolerant, easily irritated, you'll seek revenge, you'll say things which are better left unsaid. Silence has more consequences that you suspect, it determines your behaviour.

As soon as you've expressed your anger, the atmosphere will change. The air will be cleared as it were, it'll remove mutual tensions. Often you are afraid to express a feeling and you see more disadvantages than advantages. This means you're going in the wrong direction. Once you have fallen silent, it goes from bad to worse.

I wish to emphasise that unexpressed anger attracts negativity. That's how a negative spiral starts. Without realising why, you end up in the negative corner. So, appreciate what you are doing to yourself by not expressing your anger. Forewarned is forearmed.

Expressing your feelings is not just necessary for cleansing them, but also an essential part of feeling good about yourself.

In this step, I've mainly been talking about anger. I've done this because dealing with anger badly can lead to severe disadvantages. Obviously though, this approach is true of all unpleasant feelings.

Each unexpressed unpleasant feeling, pushes you into actions which don't suit you. These actions are a way of processing them, but a completely incorrect way of doing so.

Another example of unpleasant feelings which can have far-reaching consequences is rejection. You have been rejected but you don't want to feel it, let alone express it. As a result, you'll develop the tendency to reject yourself and you'll aim your unexpressed feeling at others. You're actually humiliating yourself when you do that, you're rejecting your love of yourself.

A rejection tells you that you're striving for something which your Soul doesn't want!

You see, if something suits you, you won't be rejected. By covering up your feelings of rejection, you can end up in a negative spiral and attract negativity.

My final example of non-expression is sadness. You often see people who look really unhappy. That's the result of not daring to allow their sadness in, to be felt or expressed.

Conclusion: unexpressed and unfelt unpleasant feelings determine your behaviour. This takes place at an unconscious level. So, it's important that you develop a conscious awareness of your feelings.

Maybe you find it difficult to feel, you've learned to shut feelings off to protect yourself from painful experiences. That's quite possible, but learn to break this pattern. Decide to take an act of will to allow yourself to feel and to dare to allow yourself to be affected by things.

The following list will give you some inspiration.

- Anger: fearful, panicky, dismayed, uneasy, on guard, shocked, disturbed, distrustful
- Tired: lethargic, empty, apathetic, sleepy, jaded, exhausted, defeated
- Powerless: hopeless, despondent
- Vulnerable: sensitive, insecure
- Aversion: hateful, contemptuous, horrified, disgusted
- Uncomfortable: ill at ease, embarrassed, confused
- Pain: lonely, remorseful, broken, tortured, hurt, dejected
- Tense: bad tempered, irritated, impatient, discontented, displeased
- Angry: furious, irate, outraged, enraged, revengeful
- Yearning: envious, jealous, longing
- Confused: hesitant, dismayed, puzzled, baffled, lost
- Miserable: saddened, melancholic, unhappy, downcast, disappointed
- Absent: distant, resigned, cool, indifferent, reserved, bored, alienated

If you read through this list, you will certainly feel a sense of recognition at some words. One word will affect you more and more deeply than another. This should already give you an initial idea about what you need to do. Your Soul is sensitive to words and therefore reacts immediately. At least, it does if you allow it to!

I'd like to add that it's far from enough to say that you are feeling good or bad when expressing your feelings. This might, however, be a first step towards refining what you experience.

So, start by saying: this doesn't actually feel any good and then continue. You'll arrive at your real feelings through talking. The more you talk, the easier the next step will be.

CLEANSING STEP 3: INSIGHT

The third step in clearing away ballast, clearing up your past, is looking for insights. What can the past teach you? Why is this happening to you? Which insights can you gain from the experience?

This is often a difficult task. Discussing your insights with someone is a good way to do this. Know that several insights can be linked to one experience.

How do you arrive at an insight? The first way is to continue to build on your experiences of feelings. Imagine, you feel humiliated. Why is that? What makes this experience so humiliating to you? Are you in the wrong place? Are you with the wrong people? Aren't you sticking up for yourself? Are you letting people walk all over you?

A trick which can give you clarity in this is to go back to your childhood. Look for an experience as a child or teenager in which you felt the same feeling as you do now. So, in this example of humiliation, can I remember a situation in which I experienced the same kind of feelings? Ask yourself, what could I have done differently in that situation, given the wisdom and life experience which I have today?

As a child, you naturally didn't have the same possibilities as you do now. You didn't know yet how to stick up for yourself, you had to be well behaved and to follow other people's rules, you couldn't avoid people who were close to you.

But now you're a completely different person, with a whole load more life experience, maturity and wisdom. So, apply this to your past!

If you grasp this lesson, it's possible that you'll also have insights into your recent experience of humiliation. Try the insights from your childhood out on your current situation. Apply the lessons which you've learned from your childhood to your recent experience. Would you still feel humiliated? This will teach you whether the insights were the right ones.

Maybe you didn't dare state your boundaries as a child. It's logical that you couldn't do that as a child, so there's no need to feel guilty about it now. As a child, you may also have allowed yourself to be more strongly influenced by others and assumed that others were always right. This can also lead to new realisations. You don't have to take on what someone else says. You can have your own opinions and stick up for them.

You can't change anything about your childhood experiences any more. So, don't focus on them for too long. You needed those experiences to teach yourself things today. Accept what has happened, learn your lessons and then let it be.

I'll repeat this approach again schematically:

- What feelings are you experiencing now? Give them a name and express them as well as possible.
- When and where did you have the same feeling when you were young?
- What could you have done differently then, making use of the wisdom and experience which you have today?
- Which insights have you gained from this approach?
- Apply these insights to your recent experience. As a check, how would you feel if you applied these insights?

This is the most ideal way of arriving at insights for cleansing ballast There are, however, several ways to gain insights, which I'll list for you. We're going off on a bit of a tangent here, but I think it useful to go into this in some more depth.

In the five steps above, you start from your experience of a feeling. Expressing it means that you are already gaining clarity and you may be able to reach a conclusion with insights. Linking to the past is an additional trick, but there are also other ways.

You are getting coincidences presented to you, of course, which help you understand what you are being confronted by and that is a second way to arrive at insights.

So, search for the metaphorical meaning of a particular coincidence. This will explain a lot about what you need to learn. At the end of the next chapter I'll give you an example of this.

A third way is to pay attention to any physical complaints and diseases. You can try to interpret these.

A fourth way of gaining insights is to ask yourself "what does the other show me about myself?" You may, for example, receive enormous criticism and you wonder what you need to learn from that.

It may show you something about your own behaviour; you may yourself criticise others excessively. However, it may say exactly the opposite; maybe the other is showing you what you don't dare to do yourself. Then this is confronting you with your own limitations.

The intolerances which we discussed earlier also fit into this picture. Which behaviour in others do you find really difficult to bear? Often this show you a subject which you need to deal with yourself!

A fifth way of gaining insights is to look at your experiences from the perspective of your DNA Code. Your Age Code in particular is the basis for this, but your other characteristics may also give you approaches for learning your lessons.

Think about the situation in which you, for example, felt humiliated and whether you acted in alignment with your Code. This will also give you a mass of insights.

The sixth way is to use meditation. Here you make contact with the Spirit World and you gain access to the wisdom which is present here. The Spirit World wants only to help you discover your own path. By listening in meditation to what the Spirit World has to tell you, you can arrive at innovative insights. Give it a try.

Finally, a final way to arrive at insights, is to use your own wisdom, your conscience and your experiences. You really know more than you realise. Your intuition gives you masses of information, it's a matter of being conscious of it.

You might make use of other ways of arriving at insights: astrology, tarot cards or soothsayers and mediums. I'd like to warn you about this.

Let me firstly confirm that astrology and the tarot can give you very valuable input. On the other hand, these are techniques which permit you to conclude whatever you like. Only someone who knows what they are doing can derive the correct interpretation. Unfortunately, that's not always the case.

Above all, don't confuse a statement with an insight. An insight is the change in your own actions which you want to apply in your life from now on.

A statement is the reason why you acted in a particular way in the past. A statement can lead to insights, but isn't of itself sufficient.

An insight requires an act of will, a concrete change in your behaviour! It's your answer to the question: what am I going to do differently from now on?

Let me summarize your options:

> **Seven ways of gaining insights:**
> 1. Expressing feelings
> 2. Coincidences
> 3. Physical complaints
> 4. What is the other showing me about myself
> 5. Your DNA Code
> 6. Meditation
> 7. Intuition

A very practical way of gaining insights is to look for the answers to the following questions. The basis is always whatever is happening to you:

> Why is this happening to me?
>
> How have I caused this event myself?
>
> What can I learn from this feeling I'm experiencing?
>
> Which change can I bring about in myself?
>
> Will this change lead to me experiencing the same circumstances differently from now on?

So, insight can emerge in several ways. By testing the various approaches, you can arrive at the correct conclusion. You've received some practical tools to do this and, as you know, there's only one way to learn to do something well – practise!

To make an insight your own, you have to live through the experience. Through experiencing an insight as a feeling, as a thought and as an action, it becomes an experience which you've made your own. If you only do the thinking part, then it won't stick, because you won't have "experienced" it enough. In that way, you won't have stored it in the memory that we know better as your conscience or wisdom.

So, after this little tangent, I'd like to get back to the cleansing. Let's go on to the next step.

CLEANSING STEP 4: CONSEQUENCES

The fourth step in cleansing is a difficult one. Gaining insights means that you are growing in wisdom, but applying wisdom has consequences. Many refuse to apply their insights out of fear of the consequences. If you continue to refuse to do this with your Age Code, then the Z-story which was explained earlier comes into play. But it can also be simpler, in a specific area.

For example, what if my insights tell me that I don't trust someone and I still keep in touch with them, even though I know better. After all, it's an unwritten rule that you have to like everyone, isn't it?

Well, then you're acting against your Soul. Watch out for the unwritten rules and so-called social norms. It's your own laws and your own norms and values which should determine your actions.

Take a moment to think about the consequences of your insights. Do this consciously, otherwise unconscious patterns will remain in charge. Look at what the consequences could be for yourself, your environment, your family or colleagues.

Ask yourself the question: What will happen if I now act in line with my insight and am I ok with the consequences? Accept the reality of this.

Acceptance of these consequences is a condition for being able to take the last step in the cleansing process.

CLEANSING STEP 5: ACTIONS

Taking an act of will to apply your insights in practise is the last step in the cleansing process. Then and only then will you have solved a piece of the past and will you be able to go onto the next piece.

The essence of spirituality is acting in line with your wisdom. This leads to fulfilment, motivation and contentment.

Many people get caught up in this last step, they don't have the courage to apply actual changes. In that case, the previous four steps will have been a waste of effort. Your Soul Path only unveils itself through deeds. After all, your experience leads to a feeling in which you get the confirmation that it is right and which can turn the fulfilment which this brings into the strength to carry on.

So now, with these five steps, you know how you can clear away ballast. Use the coincidences which happen to you in order to get going. Don't start from the past, but from the here and now. Then you can make a link to the past.

By going into the coincidences which happen to you today, you are treating the ballast which you need to clear away first. The Spirt World knows what has the highest priority for you and is therefore organising a suitable coincidence.

You have the choice to pick up the gauntlet and to start clearing. If you don't, then you'll get another chance, until you do decide to do so. Luckily, we have a lot of patience up here, at least much more than the average person. Be aware that you'll clear away your ballast at some point, if not now then maybe later or in your next life.

Cleansing throws another light on your Karma. Karma is a source for growing in wisdom. You've stacked up your mistakes so you can arrive at the correct conclusion at some point. This gives another perspective to Karma. In that way, it's no longer "fate", a punishment from God, but a result of your own deeds, from which you can learn your lessons, when the time is ripe.

So, Karma is a source of wisdom, a way in which to grow and to achieve your Soul wishes. By getting to grips with this, you'll feel a little bit more "whole" and a little bit more "God-like" day by day.

Cleansing fears

I've already talked about fears, primal fears, Sphere fears, fears about the consequences of acting in line with your Soul.

In essence, it boils down to you being the victim of your fears. Your actions are driven by them, not by your Soul. Your fears are often great and seem unsurmountable. You can't see any way out because of your fears, they blind you and paralyse you.

The realisation that you are the victim of your fears is the first step towards change. Accept your fears and dare to face them.

The following approach might help you with this. When you feel fear, know that you are on the right track. That will help to allow the feeling of fear in. Fear is a part of you, so don't try to escape it. Accepting your fears is the first step towards not having any more problems with them.

A first way of dealing with your fears is to burst them. Inflate your fear into a doom scenario. This will help you realise that your fear is a delusion, an illusion and it doesn't fit with reality.

Imagine, you have the primal fear of never having enough. Don't underestimate the impact of this fear, it drives you in your actions. You might restrict your spending or work extremely hard to earn as much as possible.

So, your fears drive you in behaviours which doesn't suit your Soul. How can you solve this? Well, feel the fear of never having enough, create an extremely big doom scenario, in which you have nothing left. Once you've developed your doom scenario, ask yourself the question, is this still true?

This question will bring you back down to earth. You may conclude that you'll never really not have enough, that you'll always be able to cut your coat according to your cloth, that there's a social system as a buffer and that there really isn't a reason at all to be afraid of never having enough. You'll be able to burst your own delusional bubble by realising how unrealistic it is. You may then realise that you can leave out your incorrect behaviour.

A second way of addressing your fears is to ask yourself "What if"! Imagine that you are afraid of ending up alone. This drives you to maintain contacts which may not suit you at all. You do things for other people so as not to be alone, without asking yourself whether you yourself actually want to do those things.

But "what if ..." you were to end up alone? Take a while to think about this. How bad would that be? What advantages might there be?

You might realise that you'd have much more time to yourself, that you wouldn't have to chase after other people, that you'd have the freedom to do what you really want to do.

If you then see how your fear has driven you into behaviour which doesn't fit you, you can bring about changes and adjust until you find a balance which suits you better. In that way, you can discover your Soul Path and you'll become increasingly less and less distracted by your fears.

You do this by turning your fear into knowledge. You feel literally strengthened by your insights. Insight raises your sense of self-worth, your self-love and your self-confidence.

So, you have a key in your hands to being led or not being led by your fears. You choose to be either the victim of your fears or to translate your fears into insights. In the last case, your weaknesses become your strengths.

Know that your fear emerges by not allowing feelings in. You once experienced a feeling which was too intense and that's why you never want to experience it again. You then develop a fear of experiencing that feeling and you screen your feeling off completely.

When you experience fears, ask yourself, which feeling am I refusing to allow in? Being conscious of this refusal is once again crucial. It allows you to take an act of will and to still undergo the experience, to gather up all your courage and to feel what something does to you.

You'll establish that this unpleasantness is actually not as bad as your fear had suggested. You can only experience this in a concrete situation, in a coincidence. You can't simulate this on the couch. Unveiling your Soul Path requires that you live your life consciously and are open to every experience.

I don't need to explain the importance of bursting the bubble of fears any more. You should understand by now that you need to experience the feeling to cleanse it. Fears hold you back from the cleansing process.

Once you've allowed yourself to experience your feeling, you can take the next step to insight, acceptance and change. In that way, the fear also disappears. You learn to feel instead of remaining trapped in your fear. It sounds simple and it is.

You've received a lot of information up to now about how to unveil your Soul Path and the amount of information keeps increasing. You might be wondering where to start.

Well, let coincidence play a role. Take up whatever is presented to you. Take the time to think about what is important to you today and know that you can only do one thing at a time.

If you can't decide, thumb through the book again, coincidence will help you there as well. You're bound to come across a passage which helps you at this precise moment.

Cleansing Rational Fallacies

I'd like to discuss your rational mind, your thinking. Obviously, your grey matter is a necessary thing, but it can also get you into difficulties. "Grey matter" is self-explanatory. If you use it too often you'll get a heavy head and the result is often only a grey zone. You've read something about this in earlier explanations.

You need your rational mind on a daily basis in order to be able to function in society. That's a good point, but let's put the spiritual necessity of the rational mind under a microscope.

Seen from a spiritual perspective, you need your rational mind in order to translate your feelings into the correct actions in practise. This sentence gives you the order of the Type Circle. Your rational mind helps you gain clarity about your feelings. Thinking about your feelings allows you to decide what to do.

But the rational mind is a seductive thing. Illusions, assumptions, reading thoughts, these are all things which take you further away from yourself than you suspect. That's why I can only emphasize that you need to use your feelings as a compass and then think about them.

If you experience your rational mind being in the lead, then I'll give you the following tip.

Speak and it will become clear to you.

In that way, you won't give your rational mind free rein within you. So, call a halt to your rational mind running amok, that will save you from a lot of misery. You can do that by simply saying what is occupying you. That's how you find your feelings.

An example will make this clear. Imagine that you suspect that someone is angry at you. If you continue with this assumption and give your rational mind free rein, then you could easily think of 100 reasons why this could be true.

But is it really the case? The solution is oh so easy, ask the other person if they're angry. That gives clarity and you'll find out that your rational mind often misleads you.

You're also unable to empathise with another. That's a big misunderstanding, empathy. What you suspect can only ever be based on your own experience.

The other may be showing you something, but that doesn't necessarily tell you anything about the other, only and mainly about yourself. If, for example, you think you are sensing anger in someone else, find out where the anger lies within you.

Know as well:

> *An illusion is a form of cowardice which camouflages the straightforward question.*

So, you're making assumptions instead of dealing with reality. This a very safe way of doing things, because you're always right about what you think, even if what you're thinking is completely wrong.

Your rational mind also leads you to expectations. Without saying anything, you expect the other to do this or that. That's a trap as well. See it as an exercise in power over another; if what you expect doesn't happen, you'll try to get the other to fill in your expectations, consciously or not.

An expectation is also a lack of courage to deal with something or to ask how something really is.

Illusions and expectations are themes which I could go on about for much longer. However, I've now told you the essence. Take time to reflect on your own behaviour. How are you allowing yourself to be led by illusions, when and who do you expect things of? The main point is, how could you learn to go about things differently? You'll experience this as very liberating.

Spirituality is a verb. Just working on yourself leads to change and the special thing is, if you change, this has an immediate impact on your environment.

Let's go back to your rational mind. You now know that your fears keep you from feeling. Well, your fear is a purely rational thing, an escape from feeling. You often use your rational mind as an escape route. This is not just because of your fears, but also because not having to feel is a very easy and simple escape route.

Feeling can't be controlled or managed, of course, you feel what you feel. Many people find that threatening and the simplest solution is to flee into your rational mind. There you do have some control, after all, you can think up what you like, when you like.

But if you realise that it's an escape, if you become conscious that you too often end up in your thoughts in order to not have to feel, then you can turn this around. Again, it's a matter of becoming conscious and of taking an act of will.

You could experience, for example, that your rational mind is literally and figuratively weighing your feelings down, like a ton of bricks. Then you realise that this is not the right way to do things. The importance of feelings will have become clear to you by now.

I'd like to invite you again to take some time to reflect on how you deal with your rational mind. How often do you use it as an escape? Are you afraid of feeling? Become aware of your unconscious patterns and a new world will open up to you.

I'd like to add some more examples of rational seductions. Feeling guilty is the first one. That is, by its very definition, not a feeling, but a normative pattern of thinking. You think that you're feeling guilty, because you don't live up to the demands and expectations of others.

So, the term "feeling of guilt" is a misleading one. 'I feel guilty' doesn't actually exist. By thinking that you are guilty, the experience of a feeling emerges, often feeling like a victim.

This is yet another example of how your rational mind seduces you into drawing the wrong conclusions, because you're never a victim after all.

You might react to this statement by saying that this doesn't fit your experience. Let me go into that in depth. You do regularly experience that you're a victim, that experience is a realistic one.

This can express itself as a form of numbness, not feeling anything anymore, but it can also go the other way, feeling depressed, unhappy or deprived. Whatever it is, experience it, express it and if you work on your insight, there's only one conclusion possible: you are never a victim.

You are always cause and effect, everything which happens to you has been created by you. That's a heavy conclusion, but it makes you look at yourself and take responsibility for yourself. I'll get back to this in the next chapter.

Another example of rational misunderstandings are empty promises and resolutions. These also come from your rational mind and are worthless. If you want to change something about yourself, don't turn it into a resolution, just do it now!

The usual New Year's resolutions are an example of pure stupidity. The list of resolutions for next year is as useless as can be. Just do what you resolve instead of just thinking about it and planning to do it one day.

That's how it goes with rational obstacles. Would you like another one? I'm going to put you back in front of the mirror. Are you an optimist or a pessimist?

Before you read on, do you have an answer to my question?

Well, this might be a sobering thought:

Optimism is often camouflaged pessimism.

Again, it's your thinking which is deceiving you. All too often, you only want to see the positive. Your rational mind tells you that you'll feel better that way.

But then you're escaping reality. So, what is the right attitude? See reality for what it is, both the pleasant as well as the unpleasant and accept it. Repressing unpleasant things is no good. You are taking away your chance to get clarity from your feelings about what you really want.

If you want to be an optimist or pessimist, choose the latter. You'll be closer to reality than with optimism.

Well, I've triggered your rational mind enough now. Are you a little dizzy? That's fine. Take some time to digest it all.

Just to let you know, there's more coming. I'm going to tell you about "Egotists". One last rational seduction, which I want to put into a separate paragraph.

Cleansing your Ego

"Egotists", what are they? Well, they're the people who don't succeed in finding the balance between Ego and Soul and who allow themselves to be led by the outside world instead of their inner desires.

Don't confuse an Egotist with a healthy individualist. You are of course at the centre of your world and that isn't Ego-istical. Do unto others as yourself, is often misinterpreted. First love yourself and then the other, sounds a little more insightful.

How can you love another, if you're not okay with yourself? You have to put yourself first.

The Egotist actually does the opposite. Their behaviour is determined by the outside world. It is a form of lack of self-love and of double agendas. That's because the Egotist is convinced that if they behave as others want, they'll gain something from that. It's a hidden exercise in power.

This can only lead to disappointments, because out of this Ego-behaviour, emerge expectations and that's when the dam bursts.

Still, I'd like to say yet again that you need your Ego in order to function in society. There's nothing intrinsically wrong with your Ego, it's part of you. It is, however, part of your Soul Path to realise when you are acting from your Ego and when from your Soul. It's mainly important to be aware of when you're making use of your Ego.

You can only learn this distinction through experience. Your Ego drives you into acting according to the expectations of the outside world, your parents, friends, colleagues. Often this is in conflict with what you really wish for and want.

Acting unconsciously from your Ego is not being loving to yourself. You're undergoing the temptations of the outside world, you're allowing yourself to be influenced. In addition, you tend to influence others yourself.

See your Ego as a kind of pattern, which you've internalised in order to survive, to protect yourself in order to avoid pain. You do this by copying behaviour from others. Your parents are your main examples in this. As a child, you assume that they know better, so you copy their behaviour.

Even after your childhood, you still allow yourself to be influenced by your "great" examples and want to assume their behaviour. That's not a bad experience, until you work out that this behaviour maybe doesn't suit you or until you give it a personal twist so that it becomes more part of you.

You often realise later on in life that your examples from earlier on are no longer your examples now. You'd idealised your image of others and copied them. There comes a day that you burst the bubble of your own rational mistakes.

You learn to break through the influence of the outside world and to replace it by your own behaviour and by what suits you.

So, ask yourself if your way of acting is an approach which feels really good? Again, your gut feeling is the compass which will help you differentiate who you really are.

Norms and values are also akin to this. During your upbringing, you were spoon-fed social norms, at home as well as at school and you assume that these are true. A good example is that you should like all food. It seems trivial but it's crucial. Spirituality can be found in tiny things. Why in God's name should you have to eat things that you don't like? What's the point of that?

So, it's important to discover your own norms and values and to apply them. This is how you overwrite spoon-fed norms with your own norms. Learn to disregard what others think. Acting according to your own true self gives you strength and fulfilment.

This is how you develop your own Soul Principles. These determine your boundaries and your opinions. They form the foundations for your actions. You know for yourself that you want to remain loyal to these and that you accept the consequences of applying them. They show you the way, they ensure you make distinctions.

The connection with whom and what suits you becomes strengthened in this way and what should be released, falls away by itself. This is how an essential part of your Soul Path unveils itself.

Here you're making use of your Ego in the right way. You live in a society where you don't make the rules after all. Sometimes you have to just play the game. It's a sort of role which you can play consciously. You deal with your Ego in all wisdom and you make good use of it.

Letting your Ego take control unconsciously, takes you away from who you really are. See it as inauthentic behaviour. So, learn to make the distinction. You can only do that by reflecting on yourself and asking yourself: does this really suit me? Is this what I really want to do? Am I doing this for myself or am I allowing myself to be led by others? As always, your feelings are the basis for getting clarity about this.

Growing in wisdom will also make you deal with your Ego with more wisdom. Know that's a myth that you can go through life without an Ego. That's not possible and it wouldn't help you.

The purest spiritual application of your Ego is indicating your own boundaries. You'll know that you should never do things by halves. You can use your Ego, if needs be, to make clear in a hard way where your boundaries lie. That's often the only way of making clear to another what you want!

If you do that in the right way, don't say what the other should do or not do, but state clearly where your own boundary lies which the other needs to respect.

The other then has the free choice of accepting your boundary or not. If they do, then you can continue together. If they don't, then this causes a fracture, but it's better to break up than live in uncertainty.

Practise this. It's part of the Ego-cycle which you go through in each life. In your puberty you develop your Ego, in order to apply it as a young adult.

At a given moment, often somewhere between 36 and 45, you realise that acting according to your Ego isn't right. Your Soul awakens inside and wishes to take control of your Ego.

You then only apply your Ego for indicating your own boundaries. It's your choice whether to accept this invitation.

Many choose not to accept this invitation, they stay unconscious and choose a life without insight. That's permitted and it's possible, but somewhere on your path, you'll have to learn how to deal with your Ego.

Again, it's a way of growing, gaining wisdom, discovering your authentic self and living in accordance with your Soul. As stated earlier, you are only wise if you apply your conscience in practise.

The crux of the matter is knowing which intentions inform your actions and that's what I'd like to discuss in the next chapter.

Intentions

What are intentions? See them as your inner driving force, your motives, your motivations for doing something.

All of your actions are driven by intentions. Find out for yourself how this works. Take a situation from the last few days and think about why you acted as you did. What drove you, why did you do what you did?

You're often not conscious that hidden motivations always play a role. We act automatically, but he who wants to live consciously, also reflects on his intentions. I can only emphasize that this is an essential part of your Soul Path. It may be the most important.

I'd like to make clear why. Up till now, I've left out extensive historical approaches, but now that can't be avoided. I'd like to go back in time with you, about 2000 years ago. That's when it went wrong. I'd like to refer to the story of Jesus. Yes, I know, this may be a personal hurdle for you, but it's a good example.

2000 years ago, Jesus attempted to explain what is stated in this book. He conveyed the "Message" in his way.

At that time, when there were mainly First Spheres, that wasn't obvious, but every attempt has its positive results.

Still it went pretty badly. The stories which he brought in order to make people conscious were misused by a number of his disciples. They started applying them with incorrect intentions.

Jesus offered his stories voluntarily, without force, so that anyone could make use of them out of their own free will. That's love.

Essentially two things happened after that. Firstly, there was a group which wasn't at all happy with this approach, they saw it as a threat. You can see that a loving approach can be interpreted as something quite different by others. This is a fascinating conclusion in itself.

But that is the lesser of two evils which occurred, even if that led to a crucifixion. Much worse is the misuse of his story within his own ranks.

A number of people started using the Message as a means of gaining power. On the one hand, this was for personal interests, say from the Ego, on the other hand using the motto that the ends justify the means, namely by applying force. There's nothing holy about that! Force is derived from your urges after all!

*If power rules, nothing has been learned
from what happened 2000 years ago!*

As soon as the words 'must' or 'have to' appear, people get going. People had to convert, it was the only real religion, they were obliged to convey this message further in order to win over Souls.

So, two camps emerged, one bearing love and the other bearing power. Each group thought they had the right end of the stick.

We feel the consequences of the power bearing up to the current day. I don't want to condemn anyone or anything, either about the past or the present, but I do invite you to form your own judgement, which is the basis for your own choices.

Look how the church has got itself into trouble with its complicated power structures, with the dogmas it has developed, with its obsessiveness.

That is per definition an exercise in power. Power is an incorrect intention; it's the opposite of love.

We now live in a completely different era. You're faced with the same choice as 2000 years ago. The story which I'm bringing to you now is one and the same.

I have one big question for you. Do you learn lessons from the past? Will it not become a power struggle this time? If it's your urges which are leading, then it'll lead to suffering again.

I can only add; how do you react to this story? Which camp

will you choose?

Know, there is no in-between form. You aren't a little bit powerful or a little bit loving. You choose one or the other. That has nothing to do with the fact that you're allowed to make mistakes.

As I've already said: no priests, no bishops, no cardinals, no popes, no churches either, cathedrals or basilicas, just a story, a message, which you can live with in freedom. If you choose not to, that's fine too. You have free will after all.

I can only let you experience that this would be good for you by telling the story as well as possible. That's the only correct motivation for dealing with this message. Do it for yourself or don't do it at all.

When the time is ripe, you'll start working on your Soul Path in a conscious way and you'll make progress with great strides. But that will only happen when you are ready.

That's why I'm giving you the next message, a difficult but essential one. Take your time to reflect on it:

> *If a cause has an unpleasant effect, then your own responsibility has left. You haven't taken any responsibility for your own actions.*

These two sentences require clarification, but take your time to let them sink in. The key to understanding them lies in your intentions. I'll come back to this later, but for now I'd like to continue with the power-love story.

Intentions are your drives for doing something. What motivates you to act? Basically, there are only two intentions which lead to an effect: one is power and the other is love. You take your own responsibility for this, (or not): you choose love or power.

Investigate your own intentions, arrive at insights: when are you acting out of love, when out of a need for power?

So, what is power? The answer is simple; it's exercising influence. You don't accept what is and you want to change something in another. That's why you try to influence the other and you exercise power. You don't allow the other to be free in this, you expect that the other will behave differently from now on.

Undergoing influence is also a form of power. You allow someone to exercise power over you, you adjust to the other, to their norms and expectations. That isn't what your Soul wants either.

So, what is love? Love is insight, as I've stated earlier and gives you a feeling of fulfilment. You experience that as love for yourself. Insights bring you closer to your Soul, to your authentic self. This is what your inner self is looking for.

So, loving yourself is a Soul Mission, the essence of life. How do you experience loving yourself? Go and stand in front of the mirror, preferably naked. Ask yourself the question, do I like myself, literally and figuratively? I hope that you experience a Yes, but you may find out that there's work to be done. This will wake you up to that.

Love for another is offering insights. Insights are an offer without strings, however, without force, where you give the other the freedom to do something with that insight or not. Your fulfilment doesn't come from the result of your insight for the other, but from your experience of having made your wisdom available.

Choosing love or power has far-reaching consequences. You pay a heavy price for hunger for power. You'll mainly be presented with a series of annoying presents and you might build up Soul Ballast. You often exercise power out of frustration and you don't feel that completely or express that. Your ballast can only increase in that way.

Love, on the other hand, has positive consequences, pleasant presents and you don't build up any Soul Ballast. If you're loving, then there are no unpleasant feelings to express.

Presents are always an intermediary action from the Spirit World and a result of your actions, pleasant presents from loving actions, annoying presents from exercising power. Here again you are both cause and effect, you choose which presents you receive!

What should you imagine these presents to be? Well, if you're acting in accordance with your Soul, then you'll get what you desire. If you've set your mind on a good relationship, or another job, then you'll get it.

Annoying presents are those things which don't come easily. You have the tendency to feel like a victim and to seek the cause outside yourself, but if something isn't going smoothly, then you've caused that yourself. That gives a completely different view on life.

What if someone is exercising power over you, what can you do about it? Well, then you get the chance to learn how to deal with it and to set your boundaries. It's also an exercise on your Soul Path, learning how to stick up for yourself in line with your Soul.

In that way, you prevent your ballast from growing. It doesn't give you any positive effects or presents, but you avoid annoying consequences.

The following statements may give you some inspiration:

Love ends where power begins, where looking for insights stops!

Not striving for insights is resisting your own responsibility.

If another isn't striving for insight, he may experience love as power, but that is unfair.

Stating your boundaries is pure love, unless your intention is power.

I could go into the meanings of these sentences more deeply and clarify them, but look for the meanings yourself for what is written there; when the time is ripe, you'll understand.

I'd like to emphasise one thing, the difference between sticking up for your opinion and exercising power. It's a subtle but essential difference. You could start not giving your opinion, out of fear of exercising power and that isn't the right way of acting either.

Take the following example. Your partner has changed jobs, but you soon find out that they need to do things there which can't bear the light of day. What should you do? Should you bring it to their attention or keep quiet?

You might think, if I speak, then I might be exercising power and that's not allowed, so I'll be quiet, but this is an incorrect approach. That's because it's very unloving to see your partner make a mistake and to not tell them about it.

It's necessary to give your opinion clearly and to say what you find acceptable and what not. Don't do that with the intention of influencing them, offer your insights freely. You're only sticking up for your own opinions. It's up to them what they do or don't do with them.

It's also good to say what the consequences are if they choose to do things which you find completely unacceptable. That means questioning the relationship, because someone who accepts unfair practices, won't just do that at work.

In this way, you'll arrive at the essence of the relationship via a coincidence. An open conversation will give you more clarity and also a conclusion. Accept the consequences of your opinion. Don't make any compromises, even if this has painful consequences.

This way of being may seem hard to you, but know that there's no point doing things by halves! Often a tough confrontation is needed in order to test the stability of your relationship.

In this way, you'll get more certainty about each other and you'll know that you have chosen each other because of who the other is. The truth reveals itself through this approach.

Knowing if you're acting out of power or love is the crux of your Soul Path. So, seek insight if you're acting out of love or power and do this in all areas of your life. Look at reality, at concrete situations. Don't be general in your approach, that's a form of escapism.

This is the most essential message in this book. What do you choose? If you start working in this way, a new world will open itself up to you. That's how you unveil your Soul Path. Know that you can only reap what you sow and you'll get what you deserve.

> *If a cause leads to fulfilment, then you have taken responsibility for your own actions and you are love.*

To finish off this chapter about intentions, I'd like to go back to the subject of your urges. Do you recognise yourself in this? For example, in possessiveness, a need to convince others, sexual urges, need to prove oneself, ...

I have the following message about that:

> *If an urge is focused on another, then it is pure power.*

After all, your actions are steered by your urges, so you force things in order to get your urges fulfilled and that's not right.

You always hide a hidden intention in your urges. You don't say what it's really about, but take to manipulative behaviour. The hidden intention is purely unconscious behaviour.

If you were to reveal your urge to the other, are you then exercising power? The answer is yes; you've stated your intentions, you say that you want to exercise power, but it still remains power. Knowing that you're exercising power doesn't excuse it, I don't need to explain that in any other way.

It's an annoying story, isn't it? Everyone has their urges, do I need to work through all of them, you may wonder. Well, you don't have to do anything. It's up to you to deal with this. I'm only telling you how it works and that's where my responsibility stops. The rest is up to you.

Working through your urges is part of your Soul Path. It's a matter of becoming conscious. Urges find their source in a deficiency in yourself.

Did you know that your Soul never experiences a deficiency? So, the deficiency is a result of something else: your ballast, your Karma, your fears or your rational mind.

So, how should you deal with your urges? Well, when the time is ripe and you are ready to deal with them, the first step is becoming conscious of your urge, feeling it and experiencing it.

The next step is not letting your actions be determined by your urges. I feel the urge and I do nothing, I wait until the urge fades away by itself.

But have I then removed the deficiency in myself? No, you still have work to do there, but you have prevented yourself from exercising power.

Removing a deficiency in yourself is a next step and how you do that, is actually the sum of everything in this book. You can't predict which element is lined up for you, but you can be assured that coincidences will confront you with the very aspect which is important for you now.

Know that your urge always has a cause within you; it's a form of compensation, settling the bill or an expression of your frustrations.

If you experience urges, then you can always wonder where they've come from. If you find the source and you adjust your behaviour, then the urges won't pop up as much, which brings us to the next aspect.

What about sex? Everyone experiences sexual urges, don't they? That's correct. Sex is fine, when it's experienced in freedom, it's enjoyment with one another. On the other hand, sex is and will always be just sex.

At some point, you'll take the step to transfer your sexual urges into intimacy and to attach more importance to that. Sex can be part of intimacy, but it becomes of lesser importance.

You might think, oh then I have a problem. The answer to this is yes and no. In your evolution as a Soul, this subject gets attention in 3.7, as I have already said. Your Soul wants to tackle this subject then.

However, you can get to work on this earlier. I can tell you now that sexual release, experiencing each other in every freedom, where it's not about performance, where there are no obligations and nothing has to happen, that's really "making love".

You'll experience this when you have found the right partner. It's a discovery in yourself and the other and results in a unique experience of unity. It's possible, but remember, nothing is mandatory. You either take the responsibility or you don't.

Body and Soul

Acting against your Soul also impacts your body. Your physical ailments are often a sign from which you can gain insights. I've already explained this.

Firstly, I'd like to talk about your physical balance or rather imbalance. By acting against your Soul, blockages occur in your body. You could say that you seize up energetically and physically.

Your body is a sort of Soul memory, you store your experiences in your body, in your organs and in other places. This causes difficulties. On the one hand, your physical complaints are clues from which you can gain insights, but you often don't feel the blockages.

These blockages lead to inner unease. You appreciate that there is something wrong but you aren't able to put your finger on what it is. This influences your intuitive feeling to an important extent and it becomes less pure. You'll end up getting stuck in your thinking more often as well.

Inner unease translates itself into outer unease as well. Because of this you can get out of balance. Your points of view in terms of your feelings and thoughts are not tuned into each other. You feel rushed, impatient and possibly bad tempered. These are enough arguments to pay some attention to this. Sometimes your body has a tough time of it.

Blockages are often located in your chakras, 7 energy points in your body, but your organs, joints, cartilage and muscles are also places which blockages can settle in.

You must have experienced what good it can do if you massage your head strongly or rub your eyes. These are tiny examples of blockages in your body.

You've caused these blockages through self-protection in order not to feel pain, for example. It's always a result of repeated incorrect behaviour towards your Soul.

The consequence of blockages is that they stimulate incorrect behaviour. Actually, they help you, because as a result of mistakes, you could possibly get the right insights. This is the hard way to learn.

There are techniques which can help you to break down blockages, but I don't want to go into them here. If you need them, you will definitely receive the clues you need via coincidences.

There's something which you can already start doing: talking to your body! Do this during meditation. After some practise, you'll be able to discover more than you would suspect. Start by showing your body a lot of understanding. It's had to suffer a lot at your hands. Encourage it as well. See your body as your child, that should be cherished.

In this way, you may become aware of your energetic and physical blockages and your healing process can start. Time then heals your wounds. Expressing your feelings and applying your insights are the conditions for healing. After all, then you won't need your blockage for self-protection anymore and you won't be acting against your Soul.

Another element of body and Soul are physical ailments and illness. These are signs that you're making a mistake somewhere against your Soul. Physical discomfort is the first step and if you don't listen to it, it will evolve into illness.

Metaphorical meanings of patterns of illness are a great help in gaining insight into what is happening to you. Traditional medicine definitely has its place in this. However, only take advice from someone who you feel good being around. Then you'll be able to trust the diagnosis.

It may seem contradictory that a spiritual manual defends traditional medicine. All too often, spiritual people think that alternative medicine is a must. I have only two words for that, oh dear.

You have your own free will, that's self-evident. You do what suits you, but keep being realistic, with your feet firmly on the ground. Remember, without expressing your feelings, gaining insights and committing acts of will, every intervention is useless. If you ask me, I'd opt for traditional medicine.

You run into that which you have understood, at a conscious or unconscious level. Often serious illness is a sort of turning point for people, through which their realisation grows that things need to fundamentally change.

So, illness is a good example of where science can be a good support for your spirituality. You can't have one without the other, unless you believe blindly in miracles. Know that these do happen, but keep your feet firmly on the ground.

Now I'd like to go one step further into this subject. What happens if you refuse?

Refusal

Refusal, what is that? To put it simply, you don't want to listen to your inner self, you want to impose your own free will against your better judgement.

So, what is that, your own free will? Well, see it as the sum total of things which keep you away from your own true self. You've already heard quite a few things about that.

But are there a number of additional factors which can cause difficulties here. Their impact shouldn't be underestimated and is an important part of unveiling your Soul Path.

Which elements are important here?

- Not accepting reality: Many people have the tendency to stick their heads in the sand, obscure reality or imagine that it's better than it really is. You're not accepting what is, you're deliberately refusing to see it as it is. The motto is unchanged, keep your feet on the ground.

  The consequences of not having your feet on the ground can be taken literally. How can you feel what is at stake, if you're not in the real world? How can you think that you're coming to the correct conclusions, if you are floating in a fantasy world? If you don't accept reality, you're not living in the material world and you can't gain any wisdom from concrete experiences.

- Not accepting the consequences: Here the chapter on fears is causing difficulties for you. You may develop the correct insights, but you don't dare apply them because of the possible consequences of your actions. The amazing thing is that you can never know what the consequences will be, but your doom thinking is perfectly able to create dozens of scenarios.

  On the other hand, this is correct: your actions do have consequences. Your insights could be opposite to the social norm and some people might disappear from your life as a result. The remarkable thing is that those who

fall away, don't belong in your life, but you'll only realise that when it happens. Initially this idea causes paralysis. Remember that insights without actions are pointless.
- Resistance: Resistance is the ultimate power weapon. Know that many use this as a double agenda to get what they want. An absurd anecdote will make this clear.

Once upon a time there was an eight-year-old boy who had thought up a very special form of resistance. If he didn't get what he wanted, a sweet, a toy or his favourite food, then he'd threaten his environment with the words, "Watch out, if I don't get this, I'll hold my breath".

It's ridiculous isn't it, but this was a very serious statement for this boy. It was his way of offering resistance, of blackmailing, forcing, knowing that his death would be the very worst thing that could happen to others. In this example, the resistance was clearly stated. It's transparent, but know that resistance is often hidden.

Would you like an example? Silence is a very heavy form of hidden resistance. Actually, it's a form of psychological manipulation, which many people think that they can use to achieve their aims. Silence is often used as a way of punishing those around you in order to get what you want.

Resistance is by definition not accepting what is. You are dissatisfied with reality, you don't accept it and out of your powerlessness, you develop behaviour which doesn't suit your Soul.

Actually, I wish to repeat following message:

What is, is good, otherwise it's different!

In other words, reality is always good for you, because it's what you need to experience. When I say good, I mean useful, necessary, even if it's sometimes unpleasant.
- Victim: Often you play the victim with the same intention as was just explained. You try to illicit sympathy, demand attention. In this way, you are running away from your own

responsibility and laying the cause of what has happened to you outside yourself. That's easy but you're still cause and effect.

Become aware of your attitude. Establish that you are in a victim role, experience that and then decide to step away from it. It just requires an act of will.

- Ego-behaviour: You've already learned some things about the Ego. When you act consciously according to the norms, values and expectations of others and if you don't follow your own Soul Choices against your better judgement, then this is a clear refusal.

I hope you can see the theme running through these five examples leading to refusal. Each time you actually know better and you still act differently. This is a serious sin and it can't remain without consequences.

The great theme here is consciousness. This can't be used as an excuse, but all too often you repress what you've known for a long time. Later you might think "I didn't know", but if you are honest, you'll know that that wasn't the case.

How can you find out if you are repressing something? Well, by a process of trial and error, by practising, by constantly asking questions, by standing in front of the mirror and reflecting yourself critically. It requires an act of will to develop your consciousness.

What are the consequences of refusal? Well, that depends on the seriousness of the refusal. The first little refusal won't have many consequences, but the more important the subject and the more frequent the refusal, the heavier the consequences.

This can evolve from disappointments to physical complaints and illnesses as addressed earlier. A serious illness or an accident can be the next stage and can ultimately lead to a violent death.

You may be shocked when you read that, but that's reality. You reap what you sow. Ultimately you create all of this yourself. You bear the consequences of your own actions. You bear your own responsibilities or you choose not to do so.

You may experience this as being very strict, but that's how the Greater Oneness works. It's also your inner wish to grow in wisdom by becoming conscious of your deeds. This isn't something which is enforced from outside. It's your own Soul Wish!

So how does that work with children who are seriously ill? There you need to look for the cause in their previous life, a refused act of will or not accepting consequences.

Know that the Greater Oneness relies on a law of action and reaction. Know that all of us have murdered in one of our lives, but also that we've also been murdered. Action and reaction, do you understand?

There is good news, however. You can change your fate and you do that by gaining insights, by learning from your experiences and by growing in wisdom.

Imagine that you once murdered someone and that you immediately realised that this was completely wrong. Then you gained that insight and the reaction, of being murdered yourself, didn't have to happen.

In this case you can see that you can take care of your own fate by gaining insights. You determine your future. That's good, isn't it?

I can only emphasize that there's no such thing as coincidences, you are yourself both cause and effect of everything, and I mean everything that happens to you.

This again may be shocking news, but it is a reality. From out of every coincidence you can learn, if you want to and if you're conscious, if you want to unveil your Soul Path and experience the advantages of this.

I'd like to give you an additional manual for this. How should you deal with problems? How do you deal with your own fate and create your own future? There are Degrees of Transformation for this and I'll explain this in the next chapter.

DEGREES OF TRANSFORMATION

Over the last chapters there has been a lot of explanation about what's keeping you from your Soul Path. I would like to add a following facet to this, namely solving problems by means of the Degrees of Transformation. This allows you to take your fate into your own hands and to create your own future.

This smothers the fatalistic idea of undergoing your fate. You are your own fate! It's up to you to grasp it.

How does that work? The specific aspect of the Degrees of Transformation is that you address your inner balance from the perspective of a concrete problem. Your DNA Code tells you how you act in the outside world. The Degrees of Transformation allow you to investigate your inner world.

The ultimate aim is to find a balance between the external and the internal. The importance of the Degrees of Transformation shouldn't be underestimated. See it as a spiritual view of reality.

It teaches you to approach and explain reality in a spiritually better way. This unveils your Soul Path further. The Degrees of Transformation become a way of living in this manner, no theoretical concept, but a practical manual to implement your spirituality in the material world and to adjust it.

What's my greatest problem, what keeps me awake at night? That's where it starts, from reality. Did you know that everything revolves around one single main problem for you? Determining what your main concern is, is a first step.

That's a difficult enough question in itself, but don't make it too difficult for yourself, the Degrees of Transformation allow for your humanity. After all, if you don't start with your most important problem, you'll discover what it is through the various steps.

Then there's only one basic rule, go back to the start. The system will help you arrive at the essence. As soon as you get stuck, then you'll need to start again by going through the 7 steps from scratch.

You can divide the 7 Degrees of Transformation up into 2 parts: analysing your problem and solving your problem:

Analysing your problem:

- 1ste Degree BEING self-aware: You are both cause and effect
- 2nd Degree consulting your conscience: Insight leads to enlightenment
- 3rd Degree acceptance degree: Coincidences show you the way
- 4th Degree freedom degree: You should clear away ballast from the past

Solving problems:

- 5th Degree creation degree: You can only create by trusting in the Spirit World
- 6th Degree meditation degree: Being meditative promotes contact with the Spirit World
- 7th Degree surrender degree: Only unconditional surrender leads to unity

The most striking Degree of Transformation is the 5th, the creation degree. This leads you to the next essential part of spirituality. You can take your fate into your own hands and create what suits your Soul. Choosing this consciously is the key to changing your fate.

Pure feelings are needed to mean.

Do you get this one? This is the key to creating. It'll become clearer later on.

In this way, you make your own Soul Path and you become your own road builder. The Spirit World is there to support you, but it's up to you to lay down your own tarmac.

This is an important difference to Eastern spirituality which says that you should surrender to your fate in a fatalistic way. Nothing could be further than the truth, you should take your fate into your own hands.

As a reminder, in the introductory chapter I told you that you're a speck of God. This means that you're able to create, just as God does.

A practical example is useful to make applying the Degrees of Transformation easy to understand. That's why I'll keep coming back to the following situation.

Imagine that your greatest problem is your job. You aren't motivated any more, you're tired, but you don't know what's wrong with you. How should I deal with this? What is actually my problem and moreover, how should I solve it?

The Degrees of Transformation are a handy method for getting all the answers to this. In addition, they'll help to determine what is really in line with your Soul.

1st Degree of Transformation: BEING Aware

You are yourself cause and effect.

This will hit home straightaway; you yourself are the cause of your problems. You probably tend to blame something outside yourself. The fact that you aren't feeling good at work is the fault of your boss, your colleagues or the pressure at work.

The first Degree asks you to look at yourself in the mirror and states that everything that happens to you has also been caused by you. Before going onto the next Degree, you have to understand for yourself that you are indeed the cause of everything that happens to you at work.

So, look for insights about your own role in what happens to you. Look for your own involvement, not outside yourself. In essence, you are then choosing a conscious life.

Being unconscious means rejecting your involvement, denying facts, repression due to fear, observing in a distant way, being a victim of fate. Being conscious is the acceptance of your involvement and allowing the possibility of your feelings being affected.

The 1st step is evaluating your own behaviour and perceiving your own involvement. You do that by thinking quietly and reflecting. What's happening to me and in which way am I involved in it? Be careful, this isn't about finding a guilty party in what happens to you, only your involvement.

Feeling guilty isn't actually a feeling. It's a normative pattern of thoughts, but it is one which can keep you away from your authentic self to a large extent. So, don't look for guilt, but for the link between cause and effect.

Let's take a closer look at this example: you don't feel good about yourself at work. What's your involvement in this? In the first instance, you chose this job, didn't you? You might now think, well yes, but it's not easy to find another job.

Well, that's a beautiful escape from your own responsibility.

Admit it, you and only you signed your employment contract, didn't you?

But does demotivation come from me as well, you might be asking yourself? Naturally the conditions at work determine your motivation, but again, you did choose it, didn't you?

Motivation is the result of acting in line with your Soul. So, demotivation indicates that you're doing things which aren't in accordance with your Soul Wishes. This means that the cause isn't outside yourself, but within.

An important rule is that coincidence doesn't exist. You've created everything which happens to you. Know that your problems are just possibilities for growth, things which give you the chance to become wiser.

In this way, you'll arrive at the realisation that you yourself are involved in your problem. You may not understand all the facets of this, but in the 1st Degree this isn't important as yet.

It's essential that you understand your involvement and arrive at the understanding that you really are cause and effect.

If you don't reach this conclusion, you'll still have some homework to do. It doesn't make any sense to start on the next Degree if you don't agree with the first step.

2nd Degree of Transformation: Consulting Your Conscience

Insight brings enlightenment.

Once you recognise and agree that you are involved in your problems, the next question is why is this happening to me? What do I need to learn from this?

Insight into fate, recognising the meaning of events, can be seen as your first attempt to tackle fate and to discover your Soul Path.

Of course, you are seeking spiritual insights. What was discussed earlier in the book, can help you with this.

Imagine, in our example, that you have concluded that your demotivation is meant to make you investigate what work you really want to do. This experience wants to tell you that your work maybe doesn't suit you or that you are doing it in a way that doesn't suit who you really are.

At this time, you still don't know what or how, but you realise that something isn't working and your demotivation is telling you to think about what work you are doing.

This is a general insight without a lot of detail, but for this moment that's enough. More precise insights will emerge in the next step.

It's essential in the 2nd Degree to consider that there's no such thing as coincidence. Realise that things happen to you for a reason and grasp the main theme of this meaning.

3rd Degree of Transformation: Acceptance Degree

Coincidences will show you the way.

In this 3rd Degree you look at coincidences which teach you how to see through the various aspects of your problem. By becoming aware of what happens to you, you get a lot of signs about what's causing you difficulties.

Through understanding these aspects, your acceptance of what is happening to you grows along with your awareness that it is not going as you would wish from your Soul.

Accepting the problem is the result of the insight into the meaning of coincidences and living them fully. You live them fully by going through the Type Circle; feeling them fully and expressing them is a necessity here. This will give you clarity.

By completely understanding the meaning of coincidences, you'll recognise the impact of what's happening to you and you'll realise what is occurring on the inside. Every inner intention is reflected into the outside world.

Insight into the metaphorical meanings of coincidences and physical complaints can help you in this. After all, there's no such thing as a coincidence, they're all signs.

Coincidences give you insights into yourself, your situation and the way you deal with things. This is true not just for personal aspects which have an influence but also for the process which you're going through.

Let's get back to the example. Imagine that you've always had a good evaluation over the last few years at work, but for some incomprehensible reason the tide has turned. You get the feeling that your boss is out to "get you".

If you have a problem seeing through this coincidence, then apply the previous 2 Degrees: in which way are you an involved party, cause and effect, and why is this happening to me. This can help you understand that you may be too dependent on external approval and don't have enough confidence in yourself.

Another possibility is that you're only critical of your boss or your work environment, but that you don't want to look at anything into your own affairs. Here, again, you can learn a lesson from this; you reap what you sow.

Maybe you're fighting to be seen to be right about things which don't actually affect you. Pause to think about your own responsibilities and see the boundaries of your own job. Keep away from the domain of others.

In any case, by pausing to consider coincidences you'll arrive at the conclusion that the problem is broader and deeper than you first thought. Seeing through all of these elements will clarify what it's really all about.

That's important too, because you want to solve your problem, but what you don't know, can't be solved. That's why this phase is so essential. So, don't skim over it.

If you do, then you'll run into this in the next Degrees. Then you should use a "Return to go" card.

4th Degree of Transformation: Freedom Degree

Ballast from the past needs to be cleared.

A chapter has already been devoted to clearing ballast. This will be useful here.

What do you need to clear? Ideas, behaviours, habits, emotions and frustrations which stop you living as you would like. It's a long list. It's important to tackle these elements, one by one. This takes time and insight into the drives which have determined the past.

If you skip an element, then the next step won't work. You'll find that out by experience. Changing fate is only possible by letting go of all the old patterns which haven't led to the desired result.

In the 4th Degree a stream of coincidences comes about which you can react to and which allow you to clear your ballast. Once again being aware of what's happening to you is important. This makes it a lot easier, because the subject to be dealt with is actually served to you on a platter. You only need to want to see it.

Apply the rule of 5, which was explained earlier at length, to clear ballast:

Feel – express – insight – acceptance – act of will

Be open to coincidences, feel them through and through, learn your lessons, accept them and turn them into actions.

Applying this to the earlier example, you might learn to deal with criticism and to realise how you could make use of constructive information. On the other hand, you might learn that criticism often says nothing about you but a lot about the other person.

You might learn to see through the power aspect and see at what points you take up arms and where you don't. Where do you stick to your guns without fighting and where do you assert the boundaries which you don't want to change?

In this way, you might experience your own principles and it's possible that these won't be accepted by your boss. Well, you can't change a company, nor your boss, so it's a matter of adapting or leaving. You either accept the framework in which you're working, or you don't.

By working through your past, you'll solve a lot of problems. You might arrive at the insight that your job isn't actually as bad as you thought and find out that your main problem isn't actually your main problem. By realising this, it's very probable that another subject will appear and then you can start again.

If you have cleared your past, then you can go onto the next step. But how do you know if you're finished? That's difficult to judge, so follow your feelings. Trust that it'll be fine. If there's still something which needs to be cleansed, then you'll find that out in the next stage.

5th Degree of Transformation: Creation Degree

You can only create when you trust in the Spirit World.

In order to create, you need to translate your pure feelings into an aim. Meditation and appealing to the Spirit World are a necessity here, as these take care of the presents, remember?

Trust your Soul and let yourself be led by your intuition, consult your knowing and your Guide. Meditation is a must, for that's how you can practise creating unity with the Spirit World.

What is meditation? I've discussed it earlier. Meditation is something very personal, which everyone develops in their own way. You can do this by setting up your own space, some soft music in the background, maybe burning some incense, but none of these are a must.

Breathe towards your stomach, the place where your Soul is housed. Observe your body, make yourself aware of every part of your body. Then concentrate on your breathing. Feel the air coming in and out of your body. Focus on your solar plexus, the point under your ribs at the same height as your stomach. This is where your Soul is.

Try to become calm and not to think about everyday things. If these thoughts come, just let them go. By concentrating on your breathing and keeping your focus inwards, you go into a sort of resting phase, a light trance and your meditation starts by itself.

I've already told you that your way of meditating depends on your Type. Bear this in mind and look for the ideal way for you.

Making a connection with the Spirit World is an attitude which you can teach yourself. Open yourself up to this, accept the presence of your Guide or Master, take an act of will to make contact.

The contact works via your crown, the 7th chakra. Sometimes

you can feel this contact. You can start a quiet conversation with your Guide. This is a sort of inner dialogue. You might be wondering if you aren't thinking up your answers yourself, but don't worry about this. What happens, happens.

Practising allows you to make connections with the Spirit World purely by opening yourself up to it. It's an exercise in surrendering and letting go.

Your own purity is needed to give the right information to the Spirit World which will lead to the right results.

If you've mastered meditation, you can start creating. But in order to do so, you need to know what you really want. That will take some attention. If your question isn't pure and isn't in line with what your Soul wants, then nothing will come from it.

What you ask for needs to be concrete. If you ask your Guide for help, they will just think, "I'm already helping you every day". If you ask for concrete help to gain insight into your problems at work then your Guide will say, "Finally, now I at least know what you want help with".

So, meditation is an important part of the Degrees of Transformation. Do it every day. This means that you think yourself worthwhile paying attention to. That's a beautiful form of self-love, isn't it?

In addition to mediation, a second approach is of essential importance in this Degree. Look for the answer to the following question: What do I wish to achieve with regards to my problem?

Formulate your desired result as concretely as possible. Describe your wish so that it's specific, measurable, achievable, realistic and with a time element.

The Circle of Types also gives you a helping hand. What do I think about what I'm wishing for? How does my wish feel? What do I wish to do? This will give you some additional insights, so that your wish will become even clearer.

You might now see the difference between an expectation

and a wish. Don't expect anything but determine your wish. It's good if a wish is fulfilled. An expectation has something forced, something has to happen and that doesn't work.

The following four key questions can help you to check your wish for purity and to ascertain whether what you wish to achieve is actually what you want.

First, establish what you wish to achieve and then ask yourself the following questions about it:

- 1st question: Are my intentions pure?

    The following list of statements can help you with this

    - Am I trying to prove myself?
    - Do I want to exercise influence?
    - Am I being influenced by others?
    - Are my norms and values congruent? (are they mine?)
    - Am I being driven by fear?
    - Do I have a feeling of guilt?
    - Is there an emotional connection which is causing me difficulties?
    - Why do I want this?
    - Do I have an urge to shut myself away, to be quick or hurry?

    Each of these questions can bring you back to one of the previous Degrees. You might get a broader picture of your problem like this, additional insights or you might establish that you still have something to cleanse.

- 2nd question: Is what I want to achieve meaningful and desirable, is it what my Soul really wants?

    Contemplate the point of your wish and its desirability. These may seem like simple questions, but there is more depth in the answer than you may suspect. So, take your time for this.

- 3rd question: Is what I want in line with my Age Code?

    Since your DNA Code shows the characteristics of your Soul, a check here is no more than logical. Again, this can lead to new insights and return you to previous Degrees. It'll help you get clear what you really desire.

- 4th question: Am I ready for this?

    This is the last question before you can carry on. It makes you think about the consequences of your wishes and ascertain if you accept them. Again, it's a statement which requires attention, don't make too lightly of this.

So, all of these 4 questions are very important. Here you can discover possible gaps in your desired result and you'll be turned back, as stated, to earlier Degrees of Transformation.

You might find out that you haven't cleansed all the elements, new aspects of your problem might come into play or you might find out that you didn't start with your main problem.

It's only when your wish is in accordance with your Soul, that you can start taking your fate into your own hands. Then you can determine your future and create what really suits you on the basis of your pure wishes.

What you really want is an extremely important business, but sometimes a complex one as well. That's why I'll be returning to this at the end of this chapter. But for now, let's go back to the Degrees of Transformation.

In the 5th Degree of Transformation, you're going to refine the desired result and develop it. As soon as you have the feeling that your wish is pure, you'll automatically go onto the next Degree.

6th Degree of Transformation: Meditation Degree

Being meditative promotes contact with the Spirit World.

To achieve your desired results, ask for help during your meditation every day. Don't change your question in the first instance, show your inner conviction.

To begin with you state your wish in all its facets, but after a while you "live" your question. In one single moment, you learn how to grasp what you want to achieve, in terms of contents as well as sentimentally and spiritually.

The way you ask for help from the Spirit World is also essential. Don't demand anything or give any orders. The only right way to formulate your wish is "it would be nice if..." and add "if the time is right and if God is willing".

These sentences reflect the correct attitude which is needed in order to achieve your wish. After you practise with it, you'll master it.

Through this the understanding emerges that your Soul Mission is made up of creating balance between the inner and outer world through meditation and constant contact between yourself and up there.

Being meditative is another word for developing your consciousness in reality, accepting what is, with your feet firmly on the ground and knowing what you wish for.

It's not an elevated or enlightened experience, but it is one which gives you strength and which will make you more self-confident. See it as a spiritual attitude in reality. This can allow you to go onto the next Degree.

7th Degree of Transformation: Surrender Degree

Only unconditional surrender leads to oneness.

Moving onto the 7th Degree happens again by itself. It's not an act of will, but the result of the 2 previous steps. At a given moment you experience that you are finished with it and you can let it go.

You become aware that you are part of the Greater Oneness and you contribute to this creatively. You are constantly aware of yourself, you know why and how you are doing something and what it is that you are doing, your motivation and intentions are clear. This is acting with your body, spirit and Soul in balance, in the here and now.

You don't state any conditions any more, actually it doesn't bother you anymore. That's the feeling of surrender, of letting go.

Then, quite unexpectedly, what you wished for, arrives. It just happens and gives you a feeling of bliss. Just for a moment you feel like God, because you're able to create.

Example

The Degrees of Transformation are practical instructions for taking your fate into your own hands. You might think, that's too complicated, cumbersome, longwinded or complex.

Know that the 7 steps given are a long and thorough way in which to deal with your problems. Because this might seem somewhat theoretical, I'd like to work out another example in order to further clarify the method.

The previous example was about work. Let's introduce a more delicate matter: relationships. This might be more confrontational and if that's the case, then that's an added extra. I'm working through this example as if you were experiencing it personally. This might not fit completely with your own situation, but it might strike a chord. Then you know that it's something which you also encounter, but the main aim is to let you see how you can work with the Degrees of Transformation in practise.

Imagine you're having problems in your relationship. Even worse, you can't see a way out and have decided to get a divorce. All of your other attempts haven't led to a result, this seems like the only solution.

A divorce is often a difficult process and in this case, you aren't able to arrive at an agreement together. Even worse, you've found yourself in a messy divorce. You experience this as your greatest problem.

This is a good example to let the Degrees of Transformation loose on. So, let's go through this together, step by step. How can the Degrees of Transformation help you in this process?

So, imagine, your greatest problem is your relationship and you've decided, after a long process of deliberation to finish it. This hasn't been a flawless process, however, so there's a lot of material to reflect on.

1st Degree: You Are Cause And Effect:

This seems self-evident, everyone has their part in their relationship. You can't dispute that you are an involved party. The result of the relationship is what you've made of it.

You can, of course, blame your partner entirely, but that's not right. Acknowledge that you too had a role. This conclusion doesn't say anything about the feasibility of the relationship, neither about whether you are living with the right person. It only says that you're a partial cause of what's happened in your relationship, no more and no less.

So, you're definitely an involved party. That's enough for the first Degree. I'd like to repeat again, this is not about establishing guilt. This is not a blame game. So, don't condemn yourself or the other, but look at reality as it is.

2nd Degree: Why Is This Happening To Me?:

Yes, good question, isn't it? Why is this happening? You don't have an answer to that right away, or do you? It'll lead you to a number of fundamental questions in any case. What do you want from a relationship? Who is a suitable person for you? What suits you, what doesn't? And also, how should you say your farewells? How do you close off part of your past well? How do you make a new start?

Which insights does this experience give you? Think about the start of your relationship. Where did it go wrong? Which signs did you miss? Where didn't you want to see them? Didn't want to know? Knew better but still let someone go over your boundaries or started to become too dominant yourself?

Your list of possible insights will become long very quickly and woven into your list is the main theme. Everything which happens to you has been caused by you. Since the result wasn't what you wanted, you'll have made a series of mistakes. There's nothing wrong with that, these are potential life lessons. It's a matter of dealing with them and extracting the right lessons.

Know that if you don't learn your lessons, that you'll be confronted with events which point to them, until you've understood them. If you start your next relationship without any insights, then it can only be a copy of the previous one.

To get back to our example, maybe you knew from the start that there was something wrong with your relationship, you had a lot of doubts or maybe you went into it because you thought that was the way it ought to be and so it would be good for you.

If you look back at your relationship critically, you'll certainly recognise points where you started to grow apart. You never dared to challenge the relationship, you didn't say what you wanted enough, you thought too often that things would pass and get better. Unfortunately, these were unseen chances to become aware that something was wrong.

If you list all of these, you'll find out that you didn't gain insights on various occasions, that you didn't pay attention to fundamental problems and that your current situation is only the result of the fact that you were afraid of the confrontation.

So, you don't have a messy divorce for nothing. You've avoided conflicts, so now you're getting one which you can't ignore and where you're being forced to learn to deal with the confrontation. In this way, you might learn your lesson after all.

The question why you are experiencing this quickly receives possible answers. Maybe you haven't located everything but you understand a number of possibilities. The following Degree will help you go into this in more depth.

3rd Degree: Coincidences:

These are an important phase in accepting your problem. Through the divorce process your eyes have opened and you realise that your partner is a completely different person than you thought, their true face becomes visible. Under pressure truths become apparent. This is a very confrontational experience. Why didn't you see this earlier?

You may possibly be confronted with your own true face and you might finally reflect on your own behaviour, your choices, but mainly, on what you didn't do.

Coincidences during the divorce process may confirm: I'm not suited to my partner and they aren't to me. You may for example find out that you act according to completely different norms and values, you don't believe in the same things, you have completely different visions on life.

Throughout the divorce process there will be even more coincidences which give you insights into what's happening to you. On the way to a discussion with your opposite party, there's a traffic jam and your only choice is to take a shortcut. It's busy on the shortcut as well, lots of traffic, tractors, trucks, ... your patience is being tested. You start to feel rushed, because you don't want to be late.

While you're sitting in the car you wonder what it all means. Knowing that there's no such thing as a coincidence, you try to work out why you're experiencing these coincidences. Musing about this, you may discover that you won't achieve your aim as the crow flies but that you'll come across obstacles, sometimes you'll have to take by-roads and above all, you'll need to have a lot of patience.

By accepting this you'll assume a different attitude, one which suits you better. This insight will help you accept the process, you know that it's going to take a long time and that you'll have to give things time.

Coincidences are often a mirror, a parallel with your own situation. If you know how to read these properly, a new world will open up to you.

This may take some practise, but everyone who wants to and who lives consciously, can learn how to do this. Would you like another example of this?

During the discussions about the divorce arrangements, emotions get heated. A fight starts about the smallest details and you get bogged down.

Another coincidence, why is this happening? Here you are bogged down too, realise that you too are fighting, it's not a messy divorce for nothing. Where there is a fight, there are two parties involved.

See it as a tug of war between two people. If one person decides not to join in, there's no competition.

The good thing about fighting, is that as soon as one person stops fighting, the fight also stops. In this way, you may conclude that you need to change your attitude in order to achieve a result.

But how can you approach this not fighting? Should you allow yourself to be slaughtered, call a cease fire and fatalistically await the results? This will at least make you think about your approach.

There's a simple in-between route between fighting and fleeing after all. Namely, establishing clear boundaries for yourself. It makes you think about: what do I want? Once you've determined your own line, you can defend it with the right arguments. That's a completely different thing than attacking the other person. Can you see the difference?

Laying down a boundary and defending it isn't a battle. It's a way of sticking up for yourself. It's another lesson which you're learning "thanks" to your divorce.

That's how you learn how to determine what is important to you and what isn't; which points you want to stick to and where you can be flexible. Back this up each time with good arguments.

The divorce suddenly becomes a different event. It seems like a chain of learning experiences. In this way, you'll notice that after each learning moment, you'll be a bit closer to the solution to your problem. Let me add an example to this.

Through one of the discussions you find out that you feel guilty for the failure of the relationship, because there are children involved and they shouldn't have to bear the burden of the whole story.

By recognising that you're feeling guilty, you can work through this and realise that everyone has their part to play. Furthermore, you realise that you've done your best, day in and day out.

The result is as it is. You don't need to offer any apologies, nor be sorry for your actions. You can only learn from your mistakes and take these forwards to a next experience.

How does this work for children? Don't they have to bear the brunt of the situation? How does the impact of your actions on others work here? Well, if you follow you Soul Wishes, then the results of this are the coincidences for others, things that they need to experience. It's the foundation for their life lessons, which they may or may not be able to deal with.

Be very careful, this is not a get out of jail free card to do what you like with. If you haven't consciously acted in bad faith, and you can look at yourself in the mirror in good conscience, then the consequences for the other are what they are. Know that if you're acting in line with your Soul, then you can never damage another person.

This line of argument will help you burst the bubble of your guilty feelings. Guilty feelings aren't actually feelings, they're a normative way of thinking, where you think you should live up to the norms and values of the outside world.

There is only one way of dealing with this. Learn to determine your own norms and values and act accordingly.

As you can see, a lot of coincidences provide additional insights, explain the problem, show the way to approach the problem and show you new insights.

4th Degree: Cleansing The Past:

You know how cleansing works by now. The feelings which you haven't allowed yourself to feel or put into words during your relationship play an important role here.

By being aware of this you may discover an enormous amount of anger towards your partner. At particular moments, you have covered this up under the guise of keeping the peace. But now you're becoming conscious that a lot of resentment, annoyance and frustrations have never been expressed.

So, there's work to be done. You can experience the anger, get worked up, get really angry while talking about the past to a good friend.

By putting it into words, you'll find out that you have let someone else go over your boundaries, that you haven't said stop, that you haven't stuck up for yourself. You can see the point of putting this into words, because there's more.

Suddenly you realise that you have allowed yourself to be humiliated. This is the next level which needs to be cleansed. In order to avoid humiliation, you needed to know where your boundaries were and to have acted accordingly, whatever the consequences. Another lesson: know your boundaries.

In this way layer after layer of different feelings come to the surface, loneliness, exclusion, feeling redundant, abuse, ... Think about this layer after layer and try to learn the lessons they bring.

The better able you are to cleanse ballast, the easier it will be to deal with your problem from then on. So, take the time for this.

<u>5th Degree: What Do I Want?</u>:

Slowly it becomes clear to you how you want the divorce to be arranged, how you would like to sort out the finances, how to arrange the access agreements for the children. You record for yourself how you'd like all these aspects to be.

You wonder if every wish will suit you, if your intentions are pure, if you're acting according to your DNA Code? All of these questions will help you refine your aim. Often you meditate about it until it's sorted out. By paying it so much attention so often, you make it your own. You feel every facet of it through and through.

6th Degree: Asking For Help From The Spirit World:

During meditation ask your Guide for help to achieve your wish when the time is ripe and if God is willing. Through your meditations you further refine your wishes and the points and commas are clarified. In the meantime, the discussions about the divorce continue, but you know what you want and you notice that you're starting to make progress for the first time.

Your intentions are clear. At a given moment you can let it go, when you've finished with it. Then you'll drop down into the next Degree.

7th Degree: Surrender:

By letting go, you experience that things are good as they are. It's fine if there's a solution today, it's also fine if there isn't. It doesn't matter anymore, you've finished with it.

Then, suddenly, the unexpected occurs, a final proposal is lying on the table, which you can agree to without consideration, because it's good as it is.

Afterwards, you realise that the result is completely in line with your wishes. Because of that, you experience a great deal of gratitude. You realise that you are part of the Greater Oneness and that you can rely on support if you do the right thing.

It's a fascinating example, isn't it? Hopefully, it's now clear how you can work with the Degrees of Transformation. Try it out sometime, you'll find out that it works. If you get stuck, then look for suitable support.

What Do I Want?

I'd like to discuss one more subject to finish off this chapter about the Degrees of Transformation. In the introduction to this chapter I discussed your "own free will". I want it to go as I want. But is that right? How does that work? Is what I want, really what I want? In other words, is my will in line with my Soul?

It's confusing, isn't it? Well, let me tell you something about this. You have a free will and an own will. You could describe your own will as that which you do in accordance with your Soul. Your free will is the freedom which you have in dealing with your own will.

So how come we don't know this clearly? If I want something, then I want it, don't I?

The following message may set you thinking:

Who wants what doesn't want, don't want.

That's a good one, isn't it! Think about it for a while and chop it up into bits, then it'll become clear to you. If you want something, that your inner self doesn't want, then you don't want what you want.

How do these "wills" work? The crux of the matter is which will do you listen to? To the will of your rational mind, of your Ego, your fears, your incorrect intentions or of your Soul?

Let me list the various wills together. You experience each of these as something which you really want. But only one is the real thing, a Soul Will. Tricky, isn't it?

- Ego Will: Let me give you an example straightaway: house, garden, babies! That's the social norm which you all get spoon fed with. That's the way it's supposed to be, isn't it?

    Following this will is following your Ego. You want something because you think that's how it should be, because the outside world is expecting it from you. You

177

experience the most pressure from those closest to you: parents, family, friends.

But is that what you really want? Or are you doing this to please others? It's a difficult question with a simple answer. Your Soul never doubts, but your rational mind can play tricks on you. So, think about your "Ego-Will" and try to distinguish between what you really want and what you want because that's the way it should be.

- Urge Will: I've talked about urges earlier. Then I was discussing urges aimed at others. Here, I'd like to discuss urges aimed at yourself.

The words that fit urge is 'a need to' and that's no good. Why should you have to do anything? As soon as this pops up, power isn't far behind. You'll do anything to get your urge met. The result is that you damage yourself and possibly others as well.

Think about food and drink. Overeating and over drinking is a disease which only shows a lack in yourself. It's a form of compensation. You hope that you can replace what you are missing by something else and it should be clear that this isn't very loving to yourself.

So, learn to limit yourself, learn to recognise your boundaries here as well and conclude that you don't need to eat or drink as much as you actually do. This will teach you your Soul boundaries in this area as well.

Let me be clear, don't forget to enjoy food and drink. But keep it within limits, within your own limits.

Quality or quantity, what's your policy?

You can apply this to all areas of life and to everything you do. It'll give you a lot of insights. Think about your contact with family and friends, your work, your relationship, sex, hobbies and so on.

- Rational Mind Will: You can easily translate this as wanting to be right, wanting to convince others. You can immediately sense that this is also an exercise in power. When all is said and done, you want to force your own opinion, you want others to take on your convictions.

So, you're not letting the other be free, you're not giving them a free offer when you give them your opinion and you're not giving the other the freedom to arrive at their own insight.

- Emotional Will: This starts as a result of non-expressed or non-felt-through feelings, Karma. Those feelings are somewhere in your body and want to get out. If you don't do that by expressing your feelings, they'll find another way out.

  They'll determine your behaviour. I'll repeat this again. Imagine, you have a store of anger which you haven't felt through and through. Then you'll become irritable, surly, have a short fuse, ... The store which fits the feeling will find another way out and you'll develop behaviour which doesn't fit you.

- Wild Will: The untamed will would be another good description. Don't confuse this with your intuition, we'll come back to that later.

  Your Wild Will is the consequence of impulsively wanting something without feeling, without thinking it through, just blind action. Where does this come from?

  Well, it's often the result of not accepting reality. You haven't got your feet on the ground, literally and figuratively, because of that you don't have a good sense of reality and just do anything.

  Let the lesson be clear, it's important to keep your feet on the ground. Keep living in the real world, don't cover anything up. Otherwise it'll only make you do things which you don't actually want to do.

  That's the difference to your intuition, your knowing. That's how we get to the essence: what does your Soul want?

- Soul Will: That's what you really want, what your Soul wants. So, not from your ballast, but from your authentic self.

It boils down to surrendering to what there is now. But what is that, surrender? Well, if you accept what there is and that there's no such thing as coincidence, then whatever there is now is good. Otherwise it would be different, wouldn't it?

Don't confuse surrender with fatalism. The latter is undergoing your fate as a victim. You are never that. Surrender is stepping into the moment, grabbing hold of it with both hands and trying it to let it be everything it can be.

Surrender is essentially an inner movement forwards. You step into the moment, in complete consciousness, taking the wheel yourself and determining the result yourself. You lead and if you don't do so, something else occurs, you suffer!

Let me give you another example. Each one of you is presented with a series of coincidences on a daily basis, in which you can feel what you are doing. If you live consciously, then you'll grab the change, you'll step into the feeling and you'll start looking for insights, meanings, new wisdom. Surrender is actually about getting the most out of something!

The opposite of surrender is refusal, restistance, not accepting what is. If it isn't going as "I want" then you apply tricks to get what you think you have a right to anyway. You do that by using the other "wills".

If you pause to think about this, you might recognise that you are also good at applying the other wills. However, this leads you away from your path. You're deceiving yourself!

The confusing thing is that the inauthentic wills can give you a good feeling. If you follow your Ego-Will, then it gives you a kick, it feels good. So, having a good feeling doesn't necessarily mean that this feeling is in line with your Soul.

Unfortunately, the Ego-kick is short-lived. You immediately start longing for the next experience. It's an endless street and can even be fatal.

In the next chapter, I'll explain how to deal with this. But know the following for now: you need to have experienced all the wills and to have extracted all the lessons from them before you can get to know your own Soul Will.

At the risk of repeating myself: you learn from your experiences. What you've never done wrong, you can never learn to do well. So, mistakes are a part of your path.

If you take your path in a conscious way, then you'll learn an awful lot about yourself. You'll discover, step by step, who you are and what you want.

Finally, I'd like to add this:

> *Not my will, but Your will be done,*
> *because Your will is My will!*

Do you get it? Your Souls Will is the will of the Greater Oneness. You're part of the whole after all and a whole can't want two different things. Understand that "Your will be done" only means "My will be done". Beautiful isn't it!

Unfortunately, all too often, you see me and the Spirit World as something external. On the one hand, that's correct, but on the other hand it isn't. Of course, I'm someone different, but what I'm telling you is completely in line with what you yourself want. So, you can interpret this book in two ways: as an imposed message or as your own Message.

It's up to you. Now, let's get onto the Soul Feeling, because that's the next key to unveiling your path.

RECOGNISING YOUR SOUL FEELING

Now you're able to create and take hold of your fate, there might be one more part of your Soul Path which is unclear to you. How can you find out if what you are feeling is actually a Soul Feeling? How do you know if what you want is actually a Soul Will? The answer lies in your feelings.

Feeling is a complex and even contradictory thing. Did you know that you can have a feeling which drives your actions, which contradicts what your Soul really wants? Actually, that's logical and couldn't be any other way.

Imagine, you've often experienced humiliation but you haven't allowed this feeling in, felt it through and through nor expressed it. It's stored as ballast in your body. This repressed feeling leads you to an experience in which you're humiliated, so that you get the chance to still feel and express it. Tackling this experience gives you a good feeling. Your Soul Wish isn't to be humiliated, of course; your Soul wants to liberate itself from the ballast.

So, feelings can be confusing if you can't differentiate between Soul Choices based on your Soul Feeling and feelings you experience due to ballast.

Your feelings are attracted to experiences which are useful for your Soul, but which maybe don't sit well with your inner Soul Choice. The need for humiliation could drive you to enter a relationship which doesn't actually suit your Soul.

You might learn a hard lesson in this way. After a while, sometimes decades later, there's a chance that you understand that your relationship was completely wrong and that you have been repressing your feelings for a long time.

When the time is ripe, when you are ready, then the insights will come and you'll have the feelings and express them.

There's another way as well. Applying techniques, such as regression, can help you. However, simpler ways are also possible. After all, the solution is to take up what coincidences offer you.

Know that the ballast of your Soul is like an onion consisting of many layers. You can only deal with the outer layer.

How do I know what I need to deal with? Well, coincidences steer this process. You're confronted with what is important for you at this moment. You have the free will to choose to make use of it or not.

If you don't, then we in the Spirit World, will take care of the next coincidence. Thankfully, we are very patient, because often you didn't understand it the first time.

So, make use of whatever happens to you. You can feel your feeling of humiliation fully and express it in little things, while still remaining conscious of your Soul Choices and being true to them.

The key lies in being conscious of your Soul Choices and dealing with experiences of feelings. Accepting where tiny coincidences lead you is choosing a conscious way of processing your ballast. If you don't listen to this, then you'll need to do it the hard way.

Still, one thing is clear, following your feelings is always a good way to go. Know that you choose which path you take. Both ways are good, but the hard path may take a while longer.

The impact on your ballast can only grow through this. The good news is that when you've learned a hard lesson, you won't easily forget it.

Let's take a look at the Soul Choices in detail first. They too are part of unveiling your Soul Path. How can you find out if what you want is also a Soul Choice?

The first requirement is that you keep expressing your feelings. If you go around the Type Circle and you express your feelings, you can find out what your Soul wants. This will give you clarity about the situation at least.

Contemplate your intentions as well, why do I want or do

something? By contemplating this, you'll evaluate yourself thoroughly.

To do this, you'll need to break free of the status quo, not let yourself be led by the outside world. Otherwise you won't arrive at the right insights. You'll let your self-image be obscured by the expectations of your environment.

Your DNA Code is always the main theme for your Soul Choices. So, check if your choice matches your Code.

Understand the consequences of your Soul Choice and accept these consequences. If you don't do that, then the story will stop. You then won't be able to achieve what you really want.

These tips will help you, but maybe this approach won't give you enough certainty and you'll keep on having doubts. The essential question, possibly unanswered as yet, is: do my feelings match my Soul Choice? Is what I want a Soul Choice?

Only very few can make that distinction in their feelings and to distinguish if the feelings they are experiencing are "Karma feelings" or Soul Feelings.

Thankfully there is a way for everyone to ascertain this unequivocally for themselves. Coincidences never lie and they show you what suits you and what doesn't.

The key lies again in your consciousness, seeing coincidences and interpreting them in the correct way. This may require some practise and experience. If you make an incorrect interpretation, then you'll receive a following coincidence which will make it clear to you.

Unveiling your Soul Path is done by reading coincidences. These show you the right way. But there's one other possibility, you can also do the following exercise to clear out certain questions. If you want to know if a choice is really a Soul Choice, then do the following:

- Determine the subject about which you would like clarity, for example, is my job a Soul Choice?
- Meditate for 15 minutes about this subject.
- Breathe for 10 minutes after this, in connection with your Soul. Connection means without taking any breaks, you allow your in breath to be directly followed by an out breath and then you breathe in again without pausing. Fill your stomach completely when breathing in and go as deep as you can when breathing out.
- Within 14 days you'll receive a coincidence which will give you clarity. We in the Spirit World will take care of that.

So, now you have a way which can help you gain certainty about your choices. There are a few buts, however.

Reading a coincidence properly takes some experience. You might not want to see the correct answer and your rational mind will seduce you into an incorrect interpretation, but deep inside you know how it is without any doubts. Everyone can do so, you only have to want to.

A second warning, deal with one subject at a time until you have received your clarity. If you ask several questions at the same time, you won't be able to see the wood for the trees.

So, apply wisdom to the trick offered here. Take and give the time which it needs. Easy does it.

As an extra I'll add some tips which may help discover your own self and give you more insight into your Soul Feelings:

Whatever is stopping you from applying your Age Code, is the result of an action against your Soul Feeling.

What irritates you when applying your Age Code, is often the result of your own victim behaviour.

If you're not seen or not heard when applying your Age Code, then you're exercising power.

Pause to think about each of these statements. They might be confrontational for you, but they will give you clarity. You are always cause and effect, after all.

Each of these questions means, what can I do differently? This leads to insights. Feel and express, that's how you get to know yourself better and bring your actions in line with your authentic self.

So, that's another chapter done. Don't forget to keep reading, when the time is ripe for it ...

9 MILESTONES

The unveiling of your Soul Path uncovers itself throughout your life in various phases. These steps are milestones. Knowledge about the Milestones supports your development throughout your life.

Wisdom about life and maturity can't be bought in a shop. You build this up by experiencing it yourself. It's only when the time is ripe that you can start work on some areas.

The Milestones are 9 life experiences which have an impact on your spiritual path which mustn't be underestimated. Each part has a specific function. It goes even further, it largely determines the timing in which you can take your path!

The Milestones:
- Being a child
- Adolescence
- Becoming an adult
- Work
- Relationship
- Letting go & divorce
- 50+
- 70+
- Dying

Each milestone contains a facet through which you can get to know your Soul Path. Don't start panicking just yet. You may think "Oh, then I won't have done it properly". Well, you can't change your path. You can only extract the lessons you can from it and adjust things. It's never too late to learn or to change something in your life.

Insight into the Milestones gives you insights into life. It lets you realise that life is finite and that, step by step, throughout life you are given chances to make the best of it. The total picture of your life's route may give you important insights into what you still need to address.

Children, 0 to 12

Dear Parents, this chapter is about you. I'm assuming that there aren't any children reading this book. As parents, you're often not conscious of the responsibility for guiding your child. That starts at conception.

Know that your child already has a Soul and a consciousness in the womb. It hears what you are saying, it feels what you are feeling. Above all, the child remembers. From conception onwards, a child is coloured by the experiences of their father and mother. It experiences the arguments, the love, the anger and even feels what the mother is covering up.

This is part of being a child. Know that your child chose you and that it needs this experience on their own Soul Path.

That might be a shock, but don't worry: what is, is good, otherwise it's different. So, onto the next question.

How do you bring up a child from a spiritual point of view? Well, stimulate the application of the Age Code, for the child this is the Settler.

Teach your child to deal with rules as well. Give them boundaries. You're not exercising power if your intentions are pure, but you're teaching the child to function in the outside world.

Put your own feelings into words, without any hidden expectations. If you feel angry, then it's fine to say so. If you do that with the aim of adjusting the child's behaviour, then you're going about it in the wrong way.

What a child really needs is an example. If they see from their youth onwards that expressing feelings is part of daily life, then they'll have experienced an important example, which will help them take their own path.

The main risk for parents is that they want to see their own shortcomings overcome through their children. They project what they themselves were unable to achieve on what the child should achieve.

You might also want to overprotect your child to prevent your child from experiencing what you went through as a child.

That's completely wrong. Remember, you're not your child. Your child wants to develop their own path. They don't want to copy your path, nor be protected from having their own experiences. Making mistakes is part of that. Just like everyone else, your child will learn the most from that!

Give your child the freedom to develop themselves. Give them rules to live by, but give them the space to develop as well. If you don't do that, then you'll restrict your child's growth and that will have consequences for the rest of their life. In any case, stimulate intuition and spontaneity.

You can also view it from the other side. The child has chosen these parents to learn how to escape from an attempt to be restricted. Sometimes you see that parents have no idea what to do with their child and their child is spiritually way ahead of their parents.

I can only advise you to request the DNA Code of your child. Look at the Birth Code, stimulate the Settler and offer opportunities so that the child can learn to discover their other characteristics. If you can't work it out, ask for advice.

Bringing up a child is an exciting experience, which can be seen as a confrontation with yourself. At least, that's the right approach.

Having a child doesn't have any further spiritual value, apart from learning how to let go. If you think that having a child is a Soul Wish, then you're in all probability completely wrong. Only in exceptional cases is wanting to have children a Soul Wish.

Wanting to have children is a social norm, that's the way it's supposed to be. That's why a conscious choice not to have children is often a very courageous one.

Adolescence, 12 to 18

For this age group as well, parents play an important role, but the teenager is now taking control themselves and trying to do things their way. That doesn't always go very smoothly.

Teenagers should get the freedom to develop themselves and parents can guide them in this. As stated in the chapter Age Code, the Pitfall plays the main role in this.

The teenager wants to learn the positive and negative sides of their characteristic. Parents find this difficult. However, for a child, this is necessary for their own development.

The impact of parents shouldn't be underestimated, children have to meet social norms after all. Then we're back to the chapter stifling.

On the other hand, it's up to the teenager to break free. Know that there's no such thing as coincidence and what needs to happen, should happen. Everything has a meaning after all. As we already know, you are always cause and effect.

Just like the child, the teenager needs rules to live by. These are in society as well. However, the teenager will and has to try to break them. They will learn from their own experiences.

If you prevent this learning process as a parent, then the teenager will have difficulties in their further life through not having their own frame of reference.

It's like tightrope walking on a loose wire, maintaining the rules to live by and on the other hand, allowing the teenager to fight against them.

The key lies, once again, in putting your feelings into words. As a parent, you have to give an example again. Even if it doesn't seem to be having any effect on the teenager, keep up this approach. A seed needs some time to grow and Rome wasn't built in a day either.

Realise that your teenager can only break down boundaries when they know where the boundaries are. Talk about this, help them to reach insights.

This is your task as a parent. You wanted this child, so take your responsibility for them.

What if this really doesn't work? You might have to make drastic decisions and let your child go. He who won't listen, will have to feel, there's no other way to say it.

Know that this can be a solution in the interest of your child but most of all, for yourself. This also goes against social norms, it requires a lot of courage and an act of will to follow your Soul Path in this as well.

Adult, 18 to 50

A lot happens between 18 and 50. The most important process is the Ego-cycle. From 18 onwards, you are using your Ego to make things happen in the material world. The focus lies on building up your life, not on your spiritual development.

On a spiritual level, it'd be good to become aware of your feelings from this age. See it as practising with your compass. You're already able to use your feelings to differentiate, but you'd like to implement some things in the material world first.

By using your feelings as a compass from a young age and acting in line with your feelings, you'll already have implemented several Soul Choices in the material world by the time you are 36. Stop to think about and evaluate this for yourself for a moment.

Still your actions between 18 and 36 are mainly according to the expectations of the outside world, because you haven't built up enough own references yet. There's nothing wrong with that as such, it's part of your learning process. By making mistakes, you'll find out what you do want.

Your focus lies on the positive side of your Stage Phase. You're learning to develop this into a talent. On an unconscious level, you relate this characteristic more and more to your Sphere Step. That means that you're immediately able to apply your Sphere Step in the right way from 36 onwards.

36 is a key moment which greatly determines your life. The move to Sphere Step also triggers the question: Who am I anyway? This process can take a number of years.

For whoever doesn't know the answer, you're the result of yourself. That will already give you something to think about. I can't open up your answer for you completely, unfortunately; you'll have to do that yourself.

Often you see that burn outs and midlife crises occur in the period after the age of 36. Your Soul makes you take time for yourself. At least, if you're aware that that's the intention.

It's noticeable that people start to have more setbacks to deal with from 36 onwards than at other ages.

Viewed spiritually, this is an attempt at becoming conscious. In this way, left over experiences from recent years can be processed. Through this you may be woken up, or not, and backlogged insights can emerge.

Again, you can see this as the hard way of learning lessons. It's an intervention from the Spirit World, that wants to stimulate you to choose your Soul Path.

Through this process you can learn to let go of passed on norms, from your parents for example. Your self-awareness is increasing, you have gained in maturity and wisdom in life and you now want to apply these.

Living autonomously based on your own norms and values becomes your motto. You're less easily thrown off balance, your own self-knowledge ensures stability and certainty.

From 36 onwards, the Soul starts to take over more and more from the Ego. Your inner desire for insight seems unstoppable, at least if you listen to it. You start looking at yourself in the mirror. The question who am I starts coming to the foreground more and more and that's how you arrive at your answers.

So, self-knowledge and self-awareness take control. These are often the basis for employing changes in your life. Several things no longer fit with your newly discovered identity, which may have consequences for your job or your relationship.

What was good for you between 18 and 36 is no longer relevant, other subjects appear in the foreground. The realisation grows that you're the main subject in your life.

What should you do with the difficult question, who am I? Try to formulate an answer to this for yourself. It's not easy. Let me try to help by shortening the question:

Am I? What you should see in this question, is that it's about the present tense, the here and now. Who am I now?

The following list of questions should help you further:

Am I contented? Am I happy? Am I aware of my choices? Am I okay with myself? ...

Put your answers to paper and turn the answers around. Tell yourself I am ... Slowly but surely, the image of who you are will become clear in this way.

You're already your name, your Soul, your thinking, your Ego, your rational mind, you're the sum of all of this. At one point one particular aim will have precedence over the others. By seeing the sum of the parts, you know who you are.

You're a medal, with a front and a back, with good characteristics and incredibly ugly traits. Accept the reality of this, without shame, but be aware of reality.

Still, it's a difficult question, who am I? That's why I'm giving you the following "random" example:

Who am I? I am Anthony van Dijck, a higher Soul and my Soul Mission is to freely help people discover their Soul Path. I am love, strongly confrontational, patient, understanding. I am progressive insights, seeking, finding and sharing, for whoever is open.

Who are you? Tell us, we are all ears up here! That's something else to think about, isn't it?

Know that you're the sum of parts. You're the sum of your Soul, your Ego, your fears, your Karma, your rational mind. If you recognise the parts and acknowledge them, then you're a good way towards the right answer.

Back to the Milestones. The following key moment is 45. Then the autumn of your life begins. That seems very early, doesn't it? But that's the way it is.

Then you ask yourself the question: what do I still want? If you think about it thoroughly, you'll come to the conclusion that nothing else needs to happen.

That's the moment at which your Soul has taken control over

your Ego. You experience that you've nothing else to prove. Until that age, you've been busily building things up. From now on, you can enjoy what you've achieved.

You're now able to use your Ego only if it's needed. You've developed the wisdom and maturity to do so.

Your Soul is now what is driving your actions. Realising this is the basis for experiencing fulfilment.

At a Soul level, the Soul Wish to implement your entire DNA Code develops from 45 onwards. You're going to perfectionise it using your talents. Here again several new facets will rise to the surface, which will help you unveil your Soul Path.

Still, I'd like to emphasize that you're better off not paying too much attention to it. Stay aware of your Sphere Step, that's the main task. The rest will happen by itself, when the time is ripe.

In your growth to adult-ness you develop more and more balances. The material-emotional-spiritual balance is one example of this, but also a balance between your thinking and feeling, your male and female side. You become increasingly more "whole" or "one".

You enjoy knowing the balance between your male and female sides and using it. Because of it, you become milder, riper, wiser about life.

You discover more and more the difference between real and un-real based on your own experience and you recognise this in others. You use this to make selections and you determine more and more what suits you and what doesn't.

You learn to experience that unpleasant is actually pleasant and good, a necessity for further development. Your inner strength to search for insights has only increased. You strive for love, use your strength and act in wisdom.

Real spirituality requires courage to implement the conclusions, to act from your Soul. It results in, amongst other things, a dividing line between positive and negative people.

Finally, take the time to think about which emotional choices you made at 18, 36 and 45. Meditate about them. You might not recognise your choices immediately or be too hard on yourself. Sometimes, it's in the little things.

You might come to the realisation that you have made some choices not based on your feelings. That's good as well. That's a learning moment, at least, if you still want to learn that lesson.

Work

Your work is a separate milestone. You could see it as part of becoming an adult, but given its importance, this is a separate chapter. Your work should be a Soul Choice.

Think about this statement. You spend a lot of time at work, just add up the hours.

You also gain a lot of experiences here. Saying that spirituality doesn't belong at work is therefore completely wrong.

By this I only mean that you should be able to act at work according to your true self. If you can't, this will lead to demotivation, stress and health problems.

Often, you seek the cause outside yourself. It's the pressure of work or the non-stop changes which are being implemented which cause you stress. Nothing could be further from the truth, these are only circumstances which make you reflect on yourself.

In the meantime, we have explained extensively what a Soul Choice is and how you find out if your job really suits you. Are you able to implement your DNA Code at work?

Be careful! If you think that you have the wrong job and you change work without any insight into what was wrong, then you'll end up in similar circumstances. The aim of that would be that you could still learn your lesson.

So, go and look for your insights. What can you learn from your current job? If you apply what was indicated earlier in this book, then you might conclude that you are in completely the wrong place. But there's just as great a chance that you'll get an insight that you wouldn't have got any other way.

So, do your homework thoroughly. Don't take any headlong, impulsive decisions.

Wild Wills lead to quarrels.

Then the chapter courage comes into view again, accepting the consequences of your choices. Resigning your job also entails some risks, doesn't it?

Trust your Soul. If you go for a Soul Choice, then the Spirit World will support you, even though you must do it yourself.

You'll find work which suits you. After all, you'll continue to get the experiences you need. There's no such thing as coincidence.

You've gained many tools with this book to arrive at your own insights. Go for it.

Relationship

Your relationship should be a Soul Choice as well. A lot of what's been said in the previous paragraph is also true here.

Your relationship often starts in a period that you're still very young. You don't yet have the breadth of life experience which you can call upon at a later age.

You could naturally put off your relationship until you do have that experience. Unfortunately, without doing something, you can't build up any experience in it.

That's why it's so important to follow your feelings. A big trap you can fall into, is falling in love. This is an illusion after all. Your experience of falling in love starts in your head. It brings about a series of chemical processes which make you feel euphoric.

Let's be clear that there's nothing wrong with that. Enjoy it, because that's also a part of unveiling your Soul Path. Know that it's not a gut feeling, even if you do feel butterflies in your stomach.

After a while, being in love disappears and feeling takes its place. As said earlier, you can start practising with your feelings from a young age. This is the moment to start applying this.

Definitely watch out for coincidences here. At least, if you're able to see them despite being in love. Realise that in this period you are predominantly led by the outside world and the norms which have been given to you: house, garden, babies, as already stated. Consciously dealing with this can prevent a lot of misery.

This period is very probably a long time ago for you. It may be time to have a retrospective. You'll recognise a lot as a result.

You can translate your regret about your actions into fulfilment if you learn your lesson afterwards. It's never too late to learn, whatever your age.

Then you also have your partner. You may have spent a long time trying to change them. But now you know that you've been in the chapter on power. You can only change yourself and this always affects the other.

Unveiling your Soul Path may lead to the insight that your partner isn't choosing their own path or that your paths are starting to move apart.

Then you'll arrive at the ultimate choice: accept the other as they are or leave. There is no compromise, after all. This leads us to the following milestone.

Divorcing or Releasing

And so, we arrive at the chapter divorcing or releasing. It may be a painful experience, but that doesn't have to be the case.

If work and relationship aren't Soul Choices, separate paths must follow.

Deep inside you know that, but again, your thinking takes care of at least a thousand reasons not to. The obstacle-ridden nature of your rational mind has already been discussed. Don't let yourself be distracted from your Soul Path by this.

The most difficult thing is that you can only experience how good your decision was to divorce after the event. It takes courage and perseverance. Choosing yourself is on the menu. That's probably not how you were brought up. "Love thy neighbor" is the social norm, where the addition "as you love yourself" is forgotten.

If you don't love yourself, if you act against your Soul, then you can't love someone else. Love starts with loving yourself, then love can emerge for the other and never the other way around.

Then the children. Even if having children was a Soul Choice, they need to be let go of. As I've said, children are seldom a Soul Choice.

Whatever, Soul Choice or not, letting go of children is a milestone in unveiling your Soul Path. After caring comes letting go. That's in everyone's interest, both in your own interest as well as the interest of the child.

Letting go allows you to experience how restrictive children are. Think about this for a while. How free are you if you keep holding onto the children? You might have the tendency to run away from this confrontation with yourself.

If you find this difficult, then you already have a lot of problems to which you can apply the Degrees of Transformation. You very probably carry around a lot of ballast which means that you want to hold onto the children. Your own childhood has in all probability coloured you in this way.

We call this compensatory behaviour, you want to give everything you think you have missed to your children. At least then they won't have had it as bad as I did, is the corresponding excuse. But is this the right thing to do for yourself and your child?

This will already give you something to think about. I don't want to give you all the answers here; that's your own homework. In the meantime, you've almost read all the manual.

You might have preferred to get everything on a platter, but that's not how it works. Everyone takes their own path and builds on their own experience. Only you can unveil your Soul Path, no-one else can do that for you.

That might be very tiring, but it does lead to enormous fulfilment. So, here's another last tip.

What you don't have, you can't let go of!

Oops, that will put your feet firmly back on the ground.

Fifty +

Finally, you're 50. You know a lot about life. You should have built up enough wisdom in life to fly on the wings of your own experience.

The only motto for the over 50's is experiencing fulfilment. All of life's domains should give you fulfilment.

If that isn't the case, then you still have some homework to finish. But know that you're already a few years into the autumn of your life, that you don't have to do anything anymore, the focus is on enjoying yourself.

Is that allowed, enjoying yourself? Our upbringing has put it to us in a different way. It seems that it was prohibited, but your Soul Path is only in balance if there's also a balance between enjoyment and working on yourself.

Working on yourself is often accompanied by misery, pain and unpleasant feelings, but out of that insight comes fulfilment. There's no other way to do it, unless you flee from reality, are afraid to feel or refuse to see what's happening to you.

If you've made the choice to live consciously, then know that this balance is good and enjoyment is necessary for the Soul.

Enjoyment may take precedence from 50 onwards. Your Soul really doesn't want anything else in the outer world. I can only wish that you recognise this for yourself.

From 50 onwards your focus lies on the inner world, enjoying using your life's wisdom and gaining increasingly more refined insights.

Seventy +

They're often beautiful people, the over 70's. Do you recognise them? Can you see the wisdom, the contentment, the smile about the small things in life? Seeing all of this is a pleasure.

If you don't see that then you might have problems with the idea of getting older; then you don't accept yourself. Work out whether you mask your age or experience it!

Content contemplation, that's the life philosophy of the over 70's. Nothing has to be done, but everything is still possible. That last one was a bit of a joke. It doesn't matter, because what there is, is good.

If you have this experience at 70, then you'll be looking back on your life with your eyes wide open, you'll see your mistakes and you'll know that everything went just fine. You have complete acceptance, of the past, of now and even the future.

Not everyone over 70 experiences getting older in this way. You can read in their faces how life has gone; acceptance versus defeatedness. You're the consequence of how you've lived.

The special thing about getting older is a staggering sense of time. It's like the days stream past. You get up and a little bit later, it's already evening. It's Monday and a little bit later, it's already Friday. All sense of time fades.

This is mainly because you're living in complete acceptance of what is; nothing has to happen. You're ok with what is and then time goes by without you having any sense of it.

It's a special, fine experience for which there's only one motto: carpe diem, enjoy!

Life's End

Fear of death gives lots of people difficulties. Nevertheless, there's a great certainty that you'll also be confronted with this. It's better to be prepared for it.

The way in which you die colours your life. Life's end is the ultimate surrender, letting go of earthly life. The quicker you let go of the material world and your earthly body, the easier your passing over will be.

So, accept your death, better sooner than later. Realise that dying is your last experience in life. Here again you are both cause and effect. You choose the way that you pass over.

Ultimate surrender, letting go of your earthly life, how does that work? Well, you give yourself permission to go. It's that simple.

If it's not that simple, then you grab on, you're not able to let go and dying will become the last life experience from which you can learn.

There is no manual for dying. At least, you've died hundreds of times already in previous lives and you don't appear to have got any visible damage from it.

Death isn't an end point but only a milestone, nothing more, nothing less. Your Soul has a lot of experience in dying, so it can't be that bad. It's only your ballast which could cause you difficulties.

That's everything which can keep you from your authentic self. For the Soul, it is a recurring experience after all. Only non-Soul business can make this process more difficult.

That's how I arrive at the chapter suffering.

Suffering can only become bad if you
allow yourself to be led by it.

That's one to think about, isn't it?

Suffering is painful. Pain has a cause, it's the result of not feeling something fully or not putting feelings into words which emerged through acting against your Soul.

Everyone acts against their Soul on a regular basis. You make mistakes to learn from them, that's how you grow in wisdom.

But feeling and putting your feelings into words is also essential, otherwise you're adding to the pile of "suffering". This explains the deathly struggle that many experience.

Suffering is the result of acting against your feeling, resistance, refusal. If you resist your feelings, you can't gain any insights.

Resistance is not accepting what is and, in that way, death becomes an immensely difficult path of suffering. The amount of suffering is equal to the amount of refusal during your entire life.

Acceptance of what is, gives suffering and death a reason. Suffering is a last chance to still gain insight.

This is yet another reason to work on yourself, clear your ballast, to live in line with your Soul. Know that the Soul Path keeps on going through death, so that you transform into a different state, the Soul World.

Is it better there than on Earth? Is it ruled by bliss? Well, the answer might be a bit sobering. It's just as difficult or easy as in the material world.

The Spirit World isn't a perfectly organised retirement home for the extra elderly, there are no golden spoons, no virgins as a reward. Let go of those images installed by religions. They won't help you and they aren't correct either.

So, know that the unveiling of your Soul Path is nothing other than Heaven on Earth. Once you're on the other side, your path just keeps going.

Welcome to reality. There is only one possible verdict, Heaven is everywhere! How much Heaven you experience depends on you.

And, if you accept dying, if you don't resist it, if you realise that death is also good for you (because otherwise it is different), then dying becomes an inspiring experience, in full acceptance, a conscious choice to leave your body.

That's how you make your dying into a conscious passing over.

So, now you know enough about the Milestones. I know that it consists of a mass of information and that you can't digest it all in one go. Reading this book may well be a new beginning for you.

Whenever it suits you, take a part of this book which touches you and get going on that. You can't do it all in one go, that wouldn't be realistic. You take one step at a time on your Soul Path.

I can only encourage you. Start your search, get walking and look for your path, uphill and down dale, walking sometimes, strolling at others. If you trip up, lick your wounds, learn and enjoy your insights and the view but above all, enjoy yourself.

There's just one last question left, one for you personally!

What now?

EPILOGUE

In this book, the Unveiling of your Soul Path, Anthony van Dijk has given you the manual for discovering yourself. He has placed the focus on the first three earthly Spheres and provided many practical methods, which will help you on your journey.

After the three earthly Spheres, you evolve further towards the fourth, fifth, possible sixth and seventh Sphere. What was unthinkable until recently, has become reality today. Dozens of people on earth are already in the fourth Sphere or further and the amount keeps on increasing. The Soul Growth in the material world has arrived in a new dimension because of this.

This is material for a subsequent book, that explains how you should deal with these higher Spheres and the connecting passing over fields in the material world. This makes the manual for journeying along your Soul Path longer and longer, but also clearer and more complete.

For those who are not yet as far, you can also learn a lot about yourself by knowing where your path will lead in the future. It contains a mass of ideas which you can put to use today.

Much love, strength and wisdom.

APPENDIX 1: OVERVIEW OF CHARACTERISTICS

Sphere Behaviour

<u>1st Sphere</u>

Gather as many experiences as you can in which you can implement your DNA Code and find insights into these. Your mission is to gather. Be careful, you have the tendency to take on a destructive attitude.

<u>2nd Sphere</u>

When gathering the experiences in your DNA Code, differentiate between what suits you and what doesn't and then act in accordance with your conclusion; otherwise your insights have no value. Your mission is to differentiate and to act accordingly. Be careful, you have the tendency to cover things up.

<u>3rd Sphere</u>

Differentiate for yourself by applying your DNA Code and try to help others while doing so. Offer others your insights so that they help everyone. Your mission is to elevate while offering your insights unconditionally. Be aware, you have the tendency to humiliate others.

Basic Profile: Finder - Seeker

<u>Finder</u>

Focuses on results to change the current situation, efforts need to result in personal advantage. Can be typified as the expert, wants to increase.

<u>Seeker</u>

Focuses on pushing back limits, striving for insight and expansion, thinks ahead, has a vision. Can be typified as a generalist, wants to improve themselves.

Types: Doer, Feeler, Thinker

<u>Doer</u>

Focuses on reality, looks for action and results, wants to create and make things happen in practise, using tangible concepts.

<u>Feeler</u>

Senses situations quickly and finds emotions important, adds emotional element to situations, is empathic, strives for harmonious collaboration.

<u>Thinker</u>

Strives for knowledge and insights, goes looking for Why, needs communication and sparring partners, lets themselves be led by their thoughts.

Birth Code

Each Code can be described in 3 ways:

The general description gives an initial insight into the Code

(+) gives the correct implementation of the Code.

(-) gives the incorrect implementation of the Code, an excess or lack in the (+) implementation.

1.1 Tackling

General: learn to tackle things according to your Soul Feeling.

You learn how to tackle things, how to stick up for yourself. An act of will is needed to arrive at a result. So, don't just give up. The biggest mistake you can make is doing nothing. So, act even if you don't know for certain if it is the right approach. By tackling things, you can find out, because acting leads to feeling and feeling leads to insight.

(+) You experience situations in which you need to tackle things. You grab chances and gather your strength, you initialise, you make an effort to take action and you keep going. You take to new things, you explore and dare to take risks, you create trial and error situations, you're practical and skilful in carrying things out.

(-) You dither and are hesitant, you don't take decisions; through that you splinter what there is, which leads to things breaking down. You don't take what you need out of the fear of being thought selfish, you demonstrate aimless behaviour or you take over things in a wrongful way.

1.2 Persevering

General: learn to hold onto your Soul Feeling.

You learn to keep going in sticking up for yourself and in not giving up easily. You explore whether something really suits you by keeping going at it for long enough. The biggest mistake is becoming stranded in stubbornness or giving up too easily.

(+) You experience situations in which you need to persevere until you know what you want or don't want. You don't let yourself get pushed around, you keep hold of your experiences, you want to consolidate and show that you belong and are part of things. By bringing as many things as possible together, you find out what you want to persevere in and what not. You allow yourself the time to experience something for long enough, to feel it and bear it, until you are certain about your feeling and your judgement.

(-) You can be destructive, keeping hold of the wrong people or things or business, which no longer suits you, you can pigheadedly keep going while all the time knowing better or not dare to commit out of fear of losing your freedom; through that the situation gets worse because of your own attitude.

1.3 Daring To Confront yourself and others

General: learn how to confront in line with your Soul Feeling.

You learn to confront yourself and others as well. This is necessary to defend your own interests. So, you stick up for yourself, if needs be, with powerful words and that may also be a confrontation with yourself - is my hard statement right? You'll find out through a process of confrontation. The biggest mistake you can make is avoiding confrontation, because you won't learn anything at all in that way.

(+) You experience situations in which you need to confront things. You dare to take up arms against anything which threatens you and which is unjust in your eyes, you fight for your convictions and you want to take up challenges. You dare to disagree with your environment or with your situation. You need discussions and you enjoy them. Your experience of your feelings and expressing your feelings is an important part of your experience, it's the basis for your actions.

(-) You go to battle for things which aren't worthwhile or you don't fight for things which are important out of fear of being avoided. You can easily feel rejected. You don't make any use of your experience of feelings to confront in the right way or you lose control of your emotions.

1.4 Sowing And Growing (Multiplying)

General: learn to follow your Soul Feeling with regards to sowing and growing, multiplying.

You learn to approach things with patience, to sow a seed, cherish it and give it the time to grow. You learn to appreciate that allowing things time leads to the best results. Impatience is your biggest mistake.

(+) You experience situations in which you can help yourself and your environment to grow and to improve. You want to exude affection and warmth, you want to educate, teach and encourage. You use all your experiences to help yourself and others progress and you take the time to grow. You try to win over people in this way.

(-) You run away from the responsibility for yourself or your environment, or you behave hypocritically out of fear of not being accepted. You have an exaggerated wish to adapt to others and this can lead to difficulties, misuse and extortion.

1.5: Daring To Make Mistakes

General: learn to follow your Soul Feeling through a process of trial and error.

You learn to overcome your fear of making mistakes. You naturally tend to be hesitant, because you're expecting things to go wrong, but you can only really find out by trying. So, dare to take action. If it's wrong, then learn something from it. If it's good, then that's good too.

(+) You experience situations in which you need to dare to make mistakes and you'll have to learn to accept that it can go wrong. You watch over rules and procedures, strive for order and straightforwardness, you exercise control, you want to create a framework. You take your responsibility, you are aware of your duty, you give a good example, you strive for improvement and perfection to get what you want. You'll need to learn that perfection doesn't exist.

(-) You don't act because you're afraid of making mistakes or you refuse to learn from your mistakes. You can give strong criticism of anyone who makes a mistake and behave in a dismissive way, you can take on extreme points of view and denounce tolerant attitudes in your environment.

1.6: Experiencing Emotions

General: learn to experience emotions stemming from your Soul Feeling.

You learn to experience emotions, including fear. This requires a lot of courage. But know, that if you feel fear, you're doing well. Because allowing your fear and emotions in makes them disappear so you can discover the essence. So, don't flee from your fears and don't deal with them too rationally.

(+) You experience situations in which you feel emotions and fear. Try not to run away from these by thinking or fantasising. Take a good look at your emotions and try to accept them as a part of yourself. You'll need to learn to trust in your intuition. You want to experience a climate of safety and security, you learn now not to let yourself be led by doom scenarios, you approach things carefully.

(-) You don't dare take a good look at your emotions or fears and you run away from them or let yourself be paralysed by your fears. You are oversensitive to criticism, you feel and express your anger to others. An unsafe feeling can lead to negative behaviour and powerlessness, you then start complaining about your environment, you place the blame for everything on your environment. You feel like a victim and get upset by imaginary doom scenarios.

1.7 Giving Up What Doesn't Fit

General: learn to use your Soul Feeling to let go of what you don't believe in or trust.

You learn from your experiences what suits you and what doesn't. Again and again, you are confronted by the question: Can I trust this? Should I hold onto this or let it go? The key lies in keeping what can be trusted and giving up everything else, both people as well as things.

(+) You experience situations in which you learn to let go of what you don't trust (any longer) and in which you are no longer able to believe, you eliminate from a critical and sceptical attitude. You investigate who and what you need to give up and you retain what can be trusted. You give up exaggerated dependence.

(-) Through too fast and too ill-considered action you can give up the wrong things or you refuse to give them up out of fear of loss. You may regress into negative behaviour, which can lead to passivity or resistance, you withdraw, you shut yourself off or you hang on desperately to something which doesn't suit you (any longer).

2.1: Making Your Own Choices

General: learn to use your Soul Feeling when making choices.

You learn to make your own choices, stick up for what you yourself want. That won't work the first time, but through making choices, you will ultimately arrive at your inner Soul Choice. You may possibly have to adjust your conclusion several times, until you feel that it is a real choice which suits you. Keep hold of this then and be consistent. Your biggest mistake is breaking this promise to yourself.

(+) You experience situations in which you can make your own choices autonomously. You strive for independence, you want to try everything out and experience it, you want to judge for yourself. You need variety and challenges. You investigate when, how, what and with whom you want to persevere. You strive for freedom and you're not afraid of ending up alone.

(-) You don't dare make any choices or you pursue everything desperately out of fear of missing out on something. You behave selfishly when you do so, you don't take others into account, you become belligerent and chaotic, you protest against your environment and try to prove that everything is wrong and you're right.

2.2 Valuing Possession And Values

General: learn to use your Soul Feeling to deal with value and self-worth.

You learn by experience what is really valuable to you and in that way, you develop your own sense of self-worth. Your values scale is a personal, inner evaluation and you learn to act according to your conclusions. Your biggest mistake is looking for value outside yourself and letting it depend on things over which you have no control.

(+) You experience situations in which you can enlarge your own sense of self-worth and you will ultimately have to find this in yourself. You strive to value material, emotional, intellectual or spiritual property. You want to develop personally. You attach importance to values, you want to achieve something valuable, you look for recognition but ultimately you only find that in yourself. You improve yourself by learning what is valuable and important. That's how you enlarge your own intrinsic value.

(-) Through a lack of being valued or through a low sense of your own value, you can become overly critical of others and focus on their weaknesses. You think others or yourself worthless, because of which the lack of appreciation can only increase. You don't give the right value to any forms of possession or you condemn any form of possession because of your fear of having to acknowledge your own lack of self-worth.

2.3: Differentiating Through Feelings.

General: learn to fully feel the feelings that your Soul gives you.

You learn to experience pleasant and unpleasant feelings to differentiate what you really want, what suits you. You also learn that unpleasant feelings are important and teach you things about yourself. So, learn to enjoy savouring pleasant and unpleasant feelings as well, and draw your conclusions from them.

(+) You act and judge from your feelings and gain experiences in this way. You attach importance to expressing your feelings, you want to live through them and feel them fully. You learn how to deal with positive and negative feelings, you don't avoid them and you dare to feel them fully. They give you the sense of really existing. You investigate where, when and with whom you want to create warm feelings, you want to be able to discuss your feelings and make a match between feeling and practice.

(-) You ignore your feelings, which can lead to cold behaviour, you seem to have a hard shell and you escape into your thoughts. You don't express your feelings because of the fear of not being taken seriously or you use your feelings as a means of exerting power. You can lose yourself in an excess of feelings.

2.4: Setting Boundaries

General: learn to state conditions and boundaries linked to your Soul Feeling.

You learn by experience where your boundaries lie towards the outside world. So, say where your boundaries are and experience if these are right. If a boundary doesn't feel right, adjust it until you experience it matching your inner self. Watch over this boundary, that's the only way to deal with yourself respectfully. Your biggest mistake is allowing others to set your boundaries or wanting to determine boundaries for others.

(+) You want to respect yourself and others. You treat people and things with respect and ensure others respect you too. You set conditions and state your boundaries so that you can function well and you make clear agreements. You are warm and concerned. You check others' conditions against your own Soul Feeling.

(-) You set a lot of conditions out of fear of not being seen or you don't state any conditions at all out of fear of being rejected. You don't know what you want any more and you aren't successful in determining what you want, because you focus too much on other people's expectations.

2.5: Differentiating Major From Minor Matters

General: learn how to differentiate between major and minor matters based on your Soul Feeling.

You learn what is really important to you and what isn't. By dropping the minor aspects (relinquishing) you'll feel good about yourself. Your biggest mistake is relativize important matters.

(+) You know how to distinguish between major and minor matters, you are selective and you let go of anything that's redundant, you know what's essential and important and you strive for perfection in this. You experience situations in which you can refuse things which aren't important to you, you sift through your desires and freely distance yourself from the superficial. You know how to see things in a relative light, you free yourself from the redundant, you know the value of detachment.

(-) You don't make any distinction between what's important to you or you strive for unimportant things. You can refuse all kinds of pleasures which really are important, you limit yourself too often and you can then overload yourself with guilty feelings.

2.6: Investigating

General: learn to investigate your Soul Feeling from all angles.

You learn to arrive at conclusions by investigating a situation from different angles. In that way, you can find the answers to what suits you. Use the combination of your actions, feelings and thoughts to do this. This will give you the right results. In this way, you'll learn to act in an increasingly more intuitive way and to retain what you have learned.

(+) You investigate situations critically from all angles: rationally, emotionally and intuitively, that's how you gain insights, you want to know why, you develop concepts for the Greater Oneness. You order things and broaden your horizons. You strive for insights, you want to continuously improve, you formulate your own opinions and you want to develop your own vision on life.

(-) You don't differentiate between feelings, your rational mind and your intuition or you cling to one single approach. You may experience confusion, you can be very critical of what can't be explained rationally and you feel the urge to heavily express this criticism.

2.7: Letting go the urge tot impose

General: learn how to trust your Soul Feeling without wanting to impose yourself.

You learn that it's unnecessary to demand recognition to achieve results. So, you look for a wiser way of acting than forcing, without letting others walk all over you and while still sticking up for yourself. Feel that your urge to impose isn't actually a very useful approach and let it go.

(+) You exercise authority without power, you don't look for external acknowledgement, you are self-aware and you exude authority. You don't fish for approval or acceptance, you don't have to prove yourself and you've given up your need for recognition. You allow others to do things in their own way, you guard against abuses of power. You trust in the Greater Oneness so that you can let go of your urge to impose.

(-) You are too assertive because of your fear of having no power or you are not at all assertive because your fear of using your power. You misuse your position or knowledge and you act in your own interest. You look for external recognition.

3.1 Working Together

General: learn to work together in accordance with your Soul Feeling.

You learn that working together is an unconditional offer which others can accept or reject. You also learn to feel who you would like to work with and who not. If collaborating feels good, then you can elevate yourself and others to a higher level.

(+) You want to work together and rise above contradictory elements to create a Greater Oneness, without truncating what you have learned or the other's own true self. You bear the common good in mind, you take joint initiatives and you unite points of view. You persevere in elevating yourself and others. Through working together, you lift everything up to a higher level in which everyone is valued as themselves.

(-) You don't work together, you go your own way or you force others to work with you. You can become frustrated if you aren't successful in getting others to work with you. You then don't accept that another has a free choice to collaborate or not.

3.2 Sharing

General: learn to share your Soul Feeling.

You learn to share what you have experienced and you know, that this benefits you and may be of use to others. You learn when it makes sense to share things and when it doesn't. You learn this by pausing to reflect on your experiences and by drawing conclusions from them.

(+) You share what you have gained to create extra value for everyone, through which connection and a Greater Oneness emerge. You create situations in which you can share in many ways. You improve your own position and that of others in that way.

(-) You don't share, you keep information and any gains to yourself or you try to get hold of information from others. You can misuse information to your own advantage as a means of exerting power and you can hand out misleading information to serve your own interests.

3.3 Developing Inner Balance

General: learn to create inner balance in accordance with your Soul Feeling.

You learn to achieve inner balance between your male and female side, your thoughts and feelings. You also learn to do this in relation to others and you'd like, if possible, to raise yourself and others to a higher level. You're trying to go further than the earthly and the material in this way and you are searching for deeper levels and experiences.

(+) You want to contribute so that you and your environment feel good about yourselves, you want to create and feel connection. You create an inner balance in yourself and in others via warm feelings.

(-) You only act in your own interest and you make use of power or you do nothing at all. You behave hypocritically and in your own interests. You can act obsessively towards others and become demanding. Then you forget that another has their own free will to take up your proposals or not. You can feel rejected and counteracted as a result.

3.4: Showing Comprehension

General: learn how to show comprehension in accordance with your Soul Feeling

You learn to show comprehension for yourself and others by reflecting on your experiences. In this way, you can find out what you understand and what you don't. You want to show understanding to others and in that way, elevate yourself and others to a higher level.

(+) You show understanding for your own feelings, opinions and desires as well as those of others. You strive to be compassionate and you're prepared to make yourself understandable. You promote respect, you're warm, you want to unite points of view. You try to get more insight into the motivations of yourself and others. You try to understand everything through and through and so be able to improve things. You can only do this by showing comprehension for yourself and others.

(-) You don't show any comprehension for yourself or others and you behave selfishly. You can show incorrect comprehension towards yourself by being too empathic towards others. Then you're being too self-effacing and don't dare to stick up for yourself because of your fear of the consequences. You may also try to understand and convince rationally, without showing any form of comprehension.

3.5: Elevating With Passion

General: learn to experience your Soul Feeling with heart and Soul.

You learn to act with passion and through your drive, you can raise yourself and others up to a higher level. Through your experiences you find out where your passions lie and where they don't. This leads to insights which give focus to your actions.

(+) You act with passion and drive, you strive for perfection, you work with your heart and Soul and expand your boundaries in this way. You want to act in an inspired and driven manner, you have a stimulating effect on your environment and you strive for a final target; you want to motivate and make others enthusiastic, you want to be inspirational in your work.

(-) You are passive, you don't act, you wait for others, you are paralysed or you convince others with an excess of obsessive passion, so that the other gets the feeling that they don't have a free choice any more. You create chaos because of your own behaviour.

3.6: Inner Knowing

General: learn how to follow your conscience and Soul Feeling.

You learn how to make use of your inner knowing, your intuition. By being loyal to this, it becomes clear to you what you really want and what you don't. You also want to offer your wisdom to others in this way, because by experiencing this you can develop your own wisdom and elevate others to a higher level.

(+) You act from your inner knowing and develop insights and wisdom to contribute to the Greater Oneness. You strive for inner knowing and you behave consciously. You make use of your intuition to do this. You elevate yourself and others through the insights you have gained. You take responsibility for the whole and you realise that you are part of the Greater Oneness.

(-) You deny your inner knowing, you refuse to follow your intuition and you act in a purely normative way from your thoughts or you let spirituality completely take over so that you are no longer able to function in the material world.

3.7: Unconditional Surrender

General: learn to trust your Soul Feeling and surrender to it.

You learn that applying conditions is superfluous and that loving actions can only work by not making any demands. You learn to surrender to the moment and to make maximum use of the moment, to elevate yourself and others to a higher level. You also learn to deal with your urges and to realise that these keep you from being who you really are.

(+) You're self-aware, you dare to trust and to surrender yourself, you present yourself unconditionally and that brings you and others to a higher level. You live in the here and now and you strive for oneness. You believe in yourself and in others and you show that belief can move mountains. You live in total surrender; you contribute to the Greater Oneness in this way. You exude confidence in doing so and have an inspirational impact on your environment.

(-) You don't surrender, you don't accept or you are gullible and believe and trust everyone unconditionally. You often act in a unthought through way, you have no boundaries.

Breaking Down The Code

Each Code given above consists of 2 numbers which can also be interpreted separately from one another.

<u>First Number:</u>

<u>1.x</u>

(+) Gathering: Gather experiences, both material as well as immaterial. This can be things, people, knowledge, visions, angles or insights. Gathering courage to complete tasks which require courage and effort also belongs here.

(-) Destroying: Instead of bringing together, you divide things up, chop them into bits, break them down. This can be seen in many areas. Your attention becomes diffuse, you lose your overview, you split yourself off from the group. You're torn so that you don't have any direction anymore and you don't get much done. This results in chaos where everything falls apart.

<u>2.x</u>

(+) Distinguishing: Distinguish what is important to you. Investigate what belongs to you on all fronts, both people as well as activities. Determine what is important to you or what you really need. That makes it easier to distance yourself from things that are unimportant and worthless. You also need to distinguish between people who you do and don't want to associate with.

(-) Covering up: If you're afraid to distinguish and to openly see that there are differences, then you become vague and you cover up reality. You refuse to see reality for what it is. You then don't dare to choose out of fear of provoking resistance or disapproval and you act out of fear of the consequences and of not being accepted.

<u>3.x</u>

(+) Elevating: Put effort into improving yourself and your environment, lifting it to a higher level. Make an unconditional offer to the other and apply your insights to yourself. Don't exercise any power, you are only yourself. By seeing the good characteristics of yourself and others, and by building on them, you promote good and you elevate yourself and your environment.

(-) Humiliating: You humiliate by hurting yourself or others or doing them dishonour or by underestimating yourself or others. You want to oblige others and you exercise power over them. In that way, you also humiliate yourself. Insulting, laughing at someone or embarrassing them are also forms of humiliation.

Second Number:

x.1

(+) Tackling, persevering: Get to grips with something and keep going, don't let anyone walk all over you, take forceful action. Finish what you've started, persist. Don't give up if the wind changes or due to complaints from your environment.

(-) Dawdling: you drag your feet and put things off, think up obstacles to avoid doing something, you procrastinate. You don't know what you want. You might drag your feet because of the fear of doing things incorrectly or insulting someone. Through this you never find out what you really want.

x.2

(+) Enriching: Do everything you can to enrich yourself in every possible way, materially as well as immaterially and see the value in that. Be open to new things, that's how you raise your own sense of self-worth. Keep striving to develop yourself personally. You understand the value of what you have and do.

(-) Impoverishing: You impoverish by not giving the correct value to what you have and do, both materially as well as immaterially. Through this you diminish your own sense of self-worth. You impoverish yourself by not developing yourself or being open to new things.

x.3

(+) Warmth of feeling: Allow your own feelings and emotions to flow, dare to feel them and to put them into words. Treat yourself and others with a warmth of feeling. In that way, you will achieve the most. Act from your feelings by putting into words what you experience without any hidden agenda. This gives clarity to yourself and your environment.

(-) Coldness: You're unfeeling and disinterested. You do this to protect yourself, but that doesn't get you anywhere; it only shuts you in so that others start avoiding you. You don't allow yourself to be affected by or to experience what events can bring about. This causes you to get confused and you don't know how to tackle things.

x.4

(+) Heartiness: Exude affection and heartiness for yourself and your environment. This attitude gives you the best results. Give yourself and your environment the attention needed and be patient in doing so. Don't make demands, give time and space to yourself and others. Accept everything as it is and know what you would like at the same time. Make this clear in a positive way.

(-) Heartless: You don't have any 'heart' for yourself or your environment and nothing affects you. You're harsh and you judge too quickly. Heartlessness proves that you have strongly established egotism. You don't have any comprehension or empathy, which makes any real contact impossible. You often do this because of cowardice because you're afraid of being affected yourself.

x.5

(+) Perfection: You try to do everything as fully as possible and you strive for perfection. You know that perfection doesn't exist, but you like to have everything ordered and to finish things. This makes you feel contented. You set up the necessary structures in your life to implement your perfection.

(-) Chaos: You are disorganised and chaotic. By not ordering, everything becomes a mess and you can't see the wood for the trees. You become tired, through which you're unable to get organised. To overcome the chaos, you need to structure again.

x.6

(+) Intuition: You learn to trust your intuition. By watching your intuition, you immediately feel if a person or situation is good for you or not. This all happens in a fraction of a second, because your intuition doesn't rely on thinking or rational arguments. Acting according to your intuition gives you the best results.

(-) Normative: You think and act as "you should do", according to the norm. You cling onto what you've learned from your environment in terms of norms and values. You adapt to social norms because they're safe. You become narrow minded in your thinking and acting, so that you forget to live your own life.

x.7

(+) Trust: Learn to believe and trust in all its forms. Accept that there's more between Heaven and Earth than the visible material world. Believe above all in yourself and in everything which you do and initiate and realise that you're part of a Greater Oneness. Dare to trust and act from this knowledge.

(-) Distrust: You don't believe in anything and you don't trust anyone or anything. You doubt yourself as well. You don't see any good in people or yourself anymore and you assume a pessimistic attitude. You lose sight of the Greater Oneness and you retreat into fatalism.

Q-Code

Q1- Brainstormer

Takes the lead, is dominant and assertive, takes initiative, is prepared to take risks, designs the framework, brings in ideas and concepts, gets a kick out of developing new things, is less interested in practical applications and very interested in the whole.

Q2 - Stimulator

Watches over the leader from the side line, using their conscience to do so, doesn't feel the need to be in the spotlight, is long suffering, gives very valuable input, steers when necessary, is the silent powerhouse, watches over the whole, takes the time to do so.

Q3 - Processor

Powerful implementer and strives for the best solutions within a developed framework, dots the i's and crosses the t's, is a hard worker, can take the lead within a stable domain, seems bossy to others, is a good righthand man and needs discussions with the person with final responsibility.

Q4 - Executor

Carries out what has been asked and needs clearly defined tasks, functions best through encouragement and checking and needs material advantages.

Z-Code

Z1

You are implementing your Age Code in a correct way, even if you make mistakes to learn from.

Z2

You are making mistakes in your Age Code because of refusal and fear of the consequences over a long period. An act of will to change your behaviour can bring you to Z1. A long term, incorrect implementation of your Age Code, will result in you becoming Z3.

Z3

You have refused to carry out your Age Code over a long period of time and you haven't implemented it because of fear of the consequences. The result of this is that you have difficulties with achieving your Code and finding the meaning of life. You can still find a reason for your existence in spirituality. To achieve your Soul Growth, you will have to keep trying to carry out your Age Code well. Support can help you do this. The Z3 characteristic is permanent.

Z4

You have not sought any insights from setbacks over a long period of time, your Soul Growth will remain slow.

Z5

Your constant resistance to your Age Code through negative behaviour leads to you not seeking any more insights.

C-Code And Sphere Fear

C-Code

1: The fear of bodily harm.

2: The fear of not having enough.

3: The fear of being misunderstood.

4: The fear of not belonging.

5: The fear of not being seen.

6: The fear of becoming unemployed.

7: The fear of being on your own.

8: The fear of being excluded.

9: The fear of believing in the wrong things.

10: The fear of having no place in society.

11: The fear of being restricted in your freedom.

12: The fear of being forced.

Sphere Fear

First Sphere-fear: fear of death.

Second Sphere-fear: fear of losing control.

Third Sphere-fear: fear of humiliation.

Growth Scheme Evolution Code

If you look at the growth scheme on the following page in detail, then you'll notice that the Sphere Steps have a different order than the Stage Phases. Even so, the names are identical.

You do 21 variations in each Sphere Step. These are indicated by the Stage Phases. Then you go onto the next Sphere Step.

Example: You were born with the following Code:

Sphere Step 2.2 (first column), Stage Phase 2.6 (second column) or 2.2/2.6.

This is the start of your evolution as a Seeker.

Your Evolution Code shows you your growth in wisdom. You do this in steps.

- First you work through your remaining Stage Phases in your Sphere Step 2.2/3.6, 2.2/1.7, 2.2/2.7 and 2.2/3.7.
- Then you move over to Sphere Step 2.3, where you go through all the Stage phases, starting at 2.3/1.1 up to 2.3/3.7.
- After this, you go onto 2.4 and work through all the Stage Phases.

Etcetera ...

The growth scheme will make this clear:

Growth Scheme

SPHERE STEP	STAGE PHASE
1.1 Tackling	1.1 Tackling
1.2 Persevering	2.1 Making your own choices
1.3 Daring to confront	3.1 Working together
1.4 Sowing and growing	1.2 Persevering
1.5 Daring to make mistakes	2.2 Valuing
1.6 Experiencing emotions	3.2 Sharing
1.7 Giving up	1.3 Daring to confront
2.1 Making your own choices	2.3 Feeling
2.2 Valuing	3.3 Inner balance
2.3 Feeling	1.4 Sowing and growing
2.4 Setting boundaries	2.4 Setting boundaries
2.5 Major and minor matters	3.4 Showing comprehension
2.6 Investigating	1.5 Daring to make mistakes
2.7 The urge to impose	2.5 Major and minor matters
3.1 Working together	3.5 Passionately Elevating
3.2 Sharing	1.6 Experiencing emotions
3.3 Inner balance	**2.6 Investigating**
3.4 Showing comprehension	3.6 Inner knowing
3.5 Passionately Elevating	1.7 Giving up
3.6 Inner knowing	2.7 The urge to impose
3.7 Unconditional surrender	3.7 Unconditional surrender

APPENDIX 2: THE CENTRE FOR SPIRITUAL INSIGHT

The Centre for Spiritual Insight has over 20 years of experience with personal coaching and workshops. You can find more information about this on our website. We also offer personal reports which can help you get to know yourself better.

The DNA Report is the basis for this. It represents all your Soul Characteristics: Sphere Step, Stage Phase, Pitfall, Settler, Sphere Behaviour, Basic Profile, Type, Evolution Code, Evolution Sphere Behaviour, Mars/Venus Code, Mars/Venus Trigger, Q-Code, C-Code, Z-Code. This report is requested from Sir Anthony.

The Codes are expanded with information about your Life Mission, Age Code, Pitfall Behaviour, Stress Behaviour and Correction Behaviour.

The price of a DNA Report is (4 pages): € 80 (*).

If you have requested a DNA Report, you can then request an update of your Evolution Code at a later date. In this way, you can keep track of your spiritual growth.

The price of an update in your Evolution Code is € 15 (*).

Interested? Then request a report via the website:

www.thesiranthonyfoundation.org
www.centrumvoorspiritueelinzicht.org

How an application works:
- Fill in the application form on the website.
- Transfer the amount for your request.
- Your Code will then be requested.
- The result of the request will be sent to you by mail.

(*) The prices mentioned here are valid at the time of publication of this book. It is possible that changes will be made to this; you can find these on the website.

www.ingramcontent.com/pod-product-compliance
Lightning Source LLC
Chambersburg PA
CBHW050141170426
43197CB00011B/1921